Youth Revolution

The Campaign Handbook
for Youth Organisations
Passionate about Transforming
Young People's Lives

JOHN HASSALL

First published in Great Britain 2018
by Rethink Press (www.rethinkpress.com)

Praise

'John explores the importance of working together and why we need to think more widely and more deeply about the challenges young people are facing. I am proud to say that I have seen the strategies outlined in this book actively working in the lives of the staff and students in our school, transforming their lives for the better. Highly recommended.'

David Wickes,
Deputy Headmaster, Warwick School

'Having worked for forty years around the intersection of conventional and innovative services for children and young people, I warmly welcome the creative approach John Hassall takes. He rightly places the young person at the centre of the discussion and invites us to be bold, resourceful and tireless in our pursuit of better services. Above all, he invites us to listen to young people and learn from them. This book is a highly readable and practical resource. Do you work for young people in any capacity? Do you want to be an agent for change? Then this book should be on your reading list!'

Jeannie Mackenzie
(formerly Quality Improvement Officer,
East Renfrewshire Education Department,
and author of *Family Learning: Engaging with Parents*)

'An inspiring and practical message about how we can all see young people in a new light, bring in fresh ideas and then put them into action. Youth Revolution *helps you develop a sound foundation and encourages you to think more deeply about your aims.'*

**Kerstin Friend,
Director, You Can Flourish**

'This book takes the reader on a journey that shows how, if you can find your tribe, work together and understand how young people are really living their lives, you can create dynamic solutions capable of helping young people fulfil their potential. An excellent read.'

**Jane Gurnett,
Actor, teacher and
co-founder of Act for Autism**

CONTENTS

Introduction

If you sat down right now and made a list of the kinds of challenges children and young people are facing it would take you a while. Mainstream societies across the globe often lose sight of the true impact of their actions, which means that children are dealing with some tough issues; the loss of parents, war, disability, abuse, fear, and hunger are just the tip of the iceberg. How many young people will have gone missing by the time we've travelled through this book together and mulled over the challenges it sets out? Yet young people are remarkable, aren't they?

Throughout the book I talk about mainstream societies a great deal. We all have a role to play in the way mainstream societies work. I certainly do. Whenever I mention them, I am referring to how our societies respond to many of the challenges we face by creating generic one-size-fits-all solutions. Our societies develop and deliver strategies, systems and services that they believe are capable of meeting everyone's needs across education, health and social care, and beyond. There is much to be admired in this and we need to be well organised, but dealing with our complex world in this way creates its own unique challenges. Mainstream systems are often too inflexible to recognise their own failings, and young people are often placed in a vulnerable position because these systems fall short of meeting their needs. Young people need us to think more carefully about what we do and why we do it. Those working through youth organisations and in small tribes are best placed to meet young people where they are struggling and to help them recover. This book aims to encourage a deeper and more effective connection between mainstream society and the organisations that support young people.

It's highly likely you are one of the hundreds of thousands of people around the world on a journey similar to mine. You get up in the morning willing to do whatever it takes so young people can live safe and productive lives.

I was an anxious child. I had an awful stammer. No one really connected with the fact that I found life hard. So as an adult I set out determined to feel better, but also to find out why our systems failed to recognise my difficulties and respond effectively. During the past thirty years I have worked with many young people and organisations. And I have worked across many settings: schools, colleges, psychiatric units, communities, youth centres, and residential units. I have worked in the US, the UK, and Russia, and in various roles in education, youth work, the care system, careers, and specialist outreach teams. I have learned that mainstream society goes around in circles and rarely learns from its mistakes.

There are gaps in its systems. This is why we see youth organisations operating all over the world. If you work with young people and are well organised, you are a youth organisation. But youth organisations vary considerably in size and scope. We have all come across the small community-based grassroots organisations (often charitable groups), reliant on local funding, small grants and goodwill as they support young people in their own communities. We are also aware of much larger national and international organisations, like the World Scouting Movement and UNICEF, who have expanded their work across entire continents, empowering young people and influencing international policy. Youth organisations can also be found working within our mainstream education, social care and health systems. All have a common reason for existing. Their members are passionate about seeing young people meet their potential: they see the gaps and the problems these gaps generate, and they want to do something about them.

Throughout the book I refer to these small groups of passionate individuals as 'tribes'. Tribes develop both within established youth organisations and in our local communities, and are often destined to become youth organisations in their own right. We also find them within mainstream systems such as schools, colleges or health services. They are doing some amazing and innovative work, and, by their very nature, operate in unconventional ways.

This book has been written to encourage you, as someone who wants to contribute to this work, to stop and listen.

It challenges you to think big and dare to be more radical and creative. It isn't easy generating ideas and changing the way mainstream society thinks, but it can be done. It just takes time.

Are you familiar with the story of David and Goliath? It's often used as an analogy to demonstrate how the small man, with few resources and a huge amount of luck and bravery, can confront the large and powerful corporation and win. It suggests a set of circumstances that make winning such a fight a rarity, worthy of front-page news, but there is much more to this story than first meets the eye.

We assume that Goliath was in a position of power. He clearly was, standing over seven feet tall and proven in battle, armed with all the weapons he could carry. Get close and he could cut you in half. Mainstream society can be like this. It takes few prisoners when confronted head on. But what David did was quite revolutionary. He took Goliath on, but on *his own terms*.

As David prepared to challenge Goliath, the king tried to equip David with his own armour and sword. In effect, he was expecting David to fight Goliath head on on his terms, but David refused and chose to play to his own strengths. David's backstory also played an important role. He had spent years fending off wild dogs and lions with a sling, protecting the family's sheep. He developed great courage and skill. As he approached Goliath, he stood far enough away to avoid the big man's spear and sword, and used his sling, which was as powerful as a gun. Goliath didn't really stand a chance.

There are some important lessons here. Firstly, while many youth organisations will be large enough to have a direct impact on public policy, they are still working on the fringes – so working there will make you an outsider. They expose mainstream society's faults just by existing in the first place. Confronting mainstream society head on is not always a good idea if you want to change things for the better. You'll need to think more carefully about how you challenge mainstream thinking. Secondly, you shouldn't use the same tools and weapons it uses, unless you really know how to use them! Instead, choose your own and play to your strengths. Thirdly, you need to be brave because you carry far more power than you realise. You just need to know how to use it.

Albert Einstein once said that we can't solve our problems with the same thinking that created them, so how can we think differently? I have written this book, designed to challenge the way we think about young people and to start generating new ideas and solutions, in four parts.

Part One sets the scene. We often see young people making huge progress in their lives, but we can also feel down-hearted when we see them struggle. We'll look at the gaps that appear in provision for them, and we'll consider what Rubik's cubes and young people have in common. I'll intro-duce you to the Lost Sheep Principle, and end with a close look at learning relationships and how they can promote autonomy and responsibility in the lives of the young people you work with. If we get better at connecting, we can achieve amazing things.

In Part Two, we'll explore why our own stories matter, and how we can use them to find common ground with young people. We'll examine the twelve keys to unlocking potential in young people. Finally, we'll consider what it takes to be a champion, and whether you can make the kind of impact you really want to make by staying where you are. Youth organisations thrive when those working within them know how to connect.

In Part Three, we'll look at the building blocks of the Sixty-day Challenge, and we'll explore how peaceful revolutionaries upset the odds. Creating lasting change amid challenging circumstances isn't easy. There is much to learn, and the goalposts keep moving. Revolutions can teach us how to work with limited resources, and also how great things can be achieved with the desire and the will to think in new and innovative ways. In the end, it's down to us – and that means we need to be willing to change, too. Are you ready for a challenge?

In Part Four we get practical. The Sixty-day Challenge, set out in five stages, is designed to help you focus on what change you really want to see. Sometimes we get so wrapped up in the act of working that we forget why we're doing what we're doing, and lose sight of our vital work.

That little boy I spoke about finally grew up. He learned to sit quietly and watch. He learned that he had an ability to help others see the best in themselves. He also developed an unwavering belief that when you think radically and are open to being rejected or misunderstood at times, there isn't a problem that can't be alleviated or, in many cases, solved.

If you work in a youth organisation, I commend you. I admire what you do and respect you for it. But what if you started thinking outside the box even more than you already do? What if you got better at telling young people's stories? What if your innovations, campaigns, and initiatives were better integrated into mainstream society, and the gaps between young people and mainstream thinking began to disappear? Please read this book, because I think we can do better.

PART ONE

Setting
The Scene

CHAPTER ONE

Can You See Me?

Young people present us with a conundrum.

They enter the world with wide-eyed curiosity and a determination to explore. But something happens to them as they begin to navigate the systems we've created to help develop these characteristics. Many become bogged down by the pressures of living; some rebel. They seem to lose their motivation and a little of the spark that characterised their earlier years.

Mark Twain once said that the two most important days of our lives are the day we are born and the day we find out why. Young people are born with a drive to find their place in the world, but what happens?

In the 1970s, a new craze spread around the world like wildfire: the Rubik's cube. Designed by a Hungarian architect, it is one of the biggest-selling puzzles in history. I like the Rubik's cube because it's a powerful metaphor for a young person's life.

Firstly, the Rubik's cube is *unique*. There are approximately 519 quintillion permeations. That's a lot. But the puzzle also looks familiar. We recognise the colours and they provide a point of reference. Young people's lives are like this – each is unique but has familiar points of reference.

Secondly, when most of us try to solve the puzzle, we realise it's not as easy as we might have thought. Some of us just keep moving things around hoping for the best. We're just happy when something lines up, even if it happens by accident.

Put the cube in a skilled person's hands, though, and watch how the cube transforms. I can get so far (although frequent trips to YouTube are improving my abilities), but I still need to hand it over to an expert to get the job done.

But what about the finished article? The Rubik's cube has only one successful outcome. But what constitutes success in life for one person may not constitute success for another. We spend so much of our time going for the same ideal solution and looking to manipulate young people into this 'ideal' that we miss the point.

A complete Rubik's cube is something we all recognise, but when it comes to people, what we see is not all there is. Our stories are unique and demand respect and like an uncompleted Rubik's cube we are all a work in progress.

Young people face unprecedented challenges and a future that is extremely difficult to determine. What part will they play in the future? What part can they play right now? How can we help?

I know we all live busy lives full of pressure, but just for a little while, I'd like you to stop. Please put down your mobile phone and turn off the radio. It's time for us think more carefully about who we believe young people are, what motivates them, and what they are really capable of. I'm going to tell you a couple of stories.

I once worked with a young man called David, who was approaching the end of his teenage years. I visited him at his home, where he sat cross-legged on a chair, still wearing his nightclothes. He was staring thoughtfully out of the window. The place was a little chaotic and his family was poor, but there was clearly a lot of love in the home for him and his siblings. I found out that school had been a real challenge for him. He was often too anxious to attend and didn't see the point. I rarely use the word 'genius' but I insist in this case. David was a genius.

As he spoke, I struggled to take in everything he was saying. His words had little relation to my initial questions (small talk didn't do it for him), but that didn't matter. What I heard were well-thought-out views on how to solve many of the most fascinating problems society faces. He connected ideas between various fields and domains and drew them together in brilliant and exciting ways.

His parents told me that no one seemed to recognise how clever he was. They said that his school was focused solely on him getting exam results, and that he couldn't see the point in doing the exams once he'd learned everything he wanted to. He said he saw this learning as a means to an end and not an end in itself.

He didn't know how to promote his ideas, or where his place in the world was. Such untapped potential. This meeting presented me with a real challenge. I needed to share his story and reveal his potential to those with the resources to make a real difference. Mainstream society couldn't see David properly because he wasn't able to conform socially.

Some time ago a friend asked me to chat with her son. He had attended a local private school and was readying himself for university. He was always an excellent student, and captain of the sports teams. In social situations he appeared to be the life and soul of the party, telling jokes and making everyone feel included.

But I discovered his secret. He was pretending. Behind everything was a young man who mostly just wanted to be alone. He liked people but only in small groups. He preferred to spend time reading and found all the parties draining. This wonderful young man thought it was wrong to be himself. Having the chance to tell his story was incredibly therapeutic for him.

His story became a powerful catalyst for change.

Moved by his story, his school vowed to find a way to play to the strengths of all students and help them understand themselves better. It has been a privilege to have been part of this change.

All around you and throughout the far-flung corners of the globe, young people are living their lives. They carry with them unique stories, and unseen skills and passions, just like you and I. But why do we struggle to see what is really happening in their lives?

Let's do an experiment.

I intend to prove to you that despite our best intentions, we all jump to conclusions. I'm going to tell you two stories about the same girl, Jane McKinley. Imagine we're in a professional meeting and I've been asked to tell you what I've seen so we can both decide how to respond to a request for extra support.

Scenario One

'Jane is fifteen years old and lives at home with her mum, who has been ill. She acts as a young carer, takes on lots of the responsibilities around the house, and does the shopping. When I visited her at her home, it was clear she had a lot to do but didn't complain. She's an intelligent girl, scores high on all her tests, and is respected by the teachers. Having been into her school recently, I can vouch for that. She is also creative and enjoys dance and the arts. Her friends say she's courageous because her dad left her and her mum. The turmoil had a real impact on her well-being and mental health. She's had to be brave because all this trouble made her anxious and caused her to develop a bad stammer.

'More recently, everyone who cares about her has been a little worried because she's become very angry in school and at home. She cries a lot and is becoming increasingly uncommunicative. A recent outburst at home led to a violent incident that sadly caused her mum an injury. I cannot tell you how deeply this action has affected her and how much help she needs from us right now.'

Scenario Two

'Jane is fifteen years old and lives at home with her mum. We became involved after a violent incident where her mum was hurt. Recently, Jane has been very angry and highly uncommunicative. There appears to be no way to get through to her. Really, there's no point in trying at the moment.

'She does stammer, probably triggered by all the anxiety this has caused her. (But I do wonder how much of this is her own fault.) Her advocates do say she's had to be really brave and courageous under the circumstances, although I wouldn't use these terms. On the positive side, she does like to dance, and shows signs of being creative. She is intelligent enough to get on well in school, but she doesn't focus. It's a shame she's let everything slide.'

What do you think of me now!

In the first scenario, I made a real effort to connect with Jane. I empathised with her and was advocating on her behalf.

In the second scenario, I jumped to conclusions and thought the worst of her. If you heard these stories in a meeting, what would you think?

We all jump to conclusions when presented with narratives. We might not want to, but we do. What we're actually doing is trying to put people into neat little boxes so we can easily define who they are and where they fit. But our young people don't fit into neat little boxes.

Most young people are given labels. Some are easy to carry: funny, talented, bright, intelligent. Others are not so easy to carry and can damage their chances of being successful: challenging, difficult, withdrawn, anxious, feral. Many labels are temporary, but when the word 'always' is placed in front of them, they can be difficult to shed – especially when they appear to define a particularly difficult period in a young person's life, and they want a fresh start.

Mainstream society loves labels. It also loves putting young people (including those with much more complex issues such as autism) in boxes, as though such definitions can be a focus for resources.

During the Sixty-day Challenge you'll be encouraged to think more deeply about the assumptions you make, and to delve into young people's stories. You'll also be encouraged to develop your own working hypothesis. Working hypotheses help us to avoid finalising our views and expectations. Labels, even when presented as diagnoses, should be seen as working hypotheses. They can be a helpful guide, but they also come with their own challenges, as we shall see.

A label or diagnosis can overshadow strengths or more pressing concerns. It's often wrongly assumed that the first label given or suggested is the most important. What it actually does is overshadow the things that might bring value to a young person's life, and prevents them access to better strategies and ideas.

Labels are sticky. At some point we've all spent ages trying to remove the price sticker from an item we bought, and sometimes we even damage the item in the process. Labels are hard to remove, so we should take great care when we use them. What we say today can have a long-term negative impact on an individual.

Labels make it hard to see the real person. They can be 'full-body', blocking out everything the label doesn't account for.

Labels are often just a matter of opinion. With this in mind, should we take them at face value just because someone else uses them with apparent confidence?

Young people often assume that labels and descriptions given to them are life-defining or life-affirming. I've met seventy-year-olds who believe they are stupid just because someone they trusted told them they were when they were young. (Now *that's* stupid!)

Labels can link a young person to mainstream resources more directly. Someone diagnosed with an autism spectrum disorder is far more likely to secure mainstream support than someone who has similar challenges but lacks a label. Without a label, young people can spend their whole lives 'mislabelled'. People look for the best fit, and this label often falls woefully short of providing a clear-cut understanding of their story.

Labels can help but can also divide. We will struggle to see young people for who they really are if we define them using labels. It is far better to develop an understanding of a young person's story, and to let that understanding grow (ie, to develop into a working hypothesis).

Let's return to Jane's story. Her mum has a different viewpoint.

An alternative scenario

'My Janey is fifteen and has lived with me since she was born. She is a really intelligent girl. She recently signed up for Mensa but didn't want anyone else to know. She also attended a summer scheme at a local university to explore her interest and talent in contemporary dance. She is brave and courageous because she defends me all the time. Her dad still turns up now and then and frightens us both, but she fends him off. This has made her really anxious about going out, especially at night, and she has developed a stammer and won't answer the phone. More recently it has become too much for her and she has withdrawn. She is very angry with her dad and fed up with having to explain herself at school. We had an argument. I challenged her and she pushed me. She is disappointed with her behaviour. She is a wonderful girl who deserves much more.'

What if Jane lived next door to you? Which viewpoint would you take? What stories would you tell about her? I often visit young people who hide in their homes. Some haven't seen the light of day for months.

Throughout the world there are millions of young people (aged between thirteen and thirty) who never leave their homes. Some have gradually retreated into their bedrooms, and food is left outside the door. They rarely speak to the outside world. Can you see them? As well, many families have become deeply fragmented, and have withdrawn from any support that might be available in their communities.

In Japan, this form of social withdrawal is a well-documented phenomenon called *hikikomori*. Research suggests there might be up to a million young people struggling to leave their homes throughout Japan. The problems often start in school; anxiety and social phobias develop over time. But sometimes, young adults will return from university and struggle to find work or fit in with social expectations. At this point they begin to withdraw and no one really notices.

In the UK there are similar numbers struggling to get out and about. We have a neat little box for them: NEET (Not in Education, Employment or Training). But as we know, labels can be highly explosive. Those who work in this area often unwittingly stereotype them, and suggest all NEETs are reluctant to engage. Social withdrawal is debilitating but rarely discussed.

I have met many young people who say they feel worthless, and mental health charities and support networks throughout the UK say that they hear the same thing. There appears to be a growing crisis among our young people. It has been going on for a long time. Some of our youth regularly take anti-depressants, struggle with self-harm, and even consider suicide.

Do you think the problem lies solely with them? It is not simply an issue arising from a 'personal' pathology (ie, a problem with their thinking and ability to cope), although this does play its part. Instead, it arises from a 'social' pathology, a problem with the way we as a society approach their development and document the challenges they face. It is our society that should shoulder much of the blame.

It's important for organisations with a keen interest in the well-being of young people to understand that many of the problems they experience don't begin within them. Society plays a much bigger part in how an individual's vulnerabilities are laid bare. Our systems struggle to empathise. That's why we need to tell their stories more effectively.

Many years ago, I worked as a careers adviser, and offered advice and guidance. Advice is easy. Careers advisers take on board what the young person is asking, normally in a short interview. Then we give them an action plan. The rest is up to them. But guidance goes a lot deeper. There is no way we can guide people and support them unless we really connect to and understand their stories. We don't have to agree with their decisions all the time – but we do need to connect.

If you have no interest in understanding where they're coming from and discovering what drives them forward, then do something else for a living! Young people need adults and organisations who see their work as a vocation and not just a job. Young people are not impressed by the latter.

Understanding why an individual has come to a particular point in their life takes a lot of work. You must be intrinsically motivated to make a difference and tell their story in a way that helps them move forward more positively.

Several key themes have emerged in my discussions with young people over the past few years. There are things they want us to know.

⊕ **They want us to stop underestimating them.** 'You don't appear to expect much from us so we stop expecting much from ourselves. You need to expect much more but you should also be prepared to show us how to get there. We know when you don't care.' David, aged thirteen

⊙ **They want us to play to their strengths because they are entering adulthood having no idea what they are good at.** 'Change things so we can find out what we are good at and understand ourselves better. Let us try lots of things, not just the things you say.' Jo, aged fourteen

⊙ **They want us to think more deeply about what we want them to learn and why.** 'So much of what you teach me has nothing to do with real life. Aren't there more important things for us to learn?' Annabelle, aged fifteen

⊙ **They want us not to think the worst of them.** 'I am not my behaviour. I want you to see past it and find out why. I am a human being just like you and feel upset when you do that. Are you surprised when I stop caring?' Jack, aged sixteen

⊙ **They want us to know they are intrinsically motivated and often resent the carrot and stick.** 'We are trying to do the right thing but need help setting our own boundaries and need you to help us stick to them.' Tyrone, aged seventeen

⊙ **They want us to know they are under huge pressure at school.** 'We are under loads of pressure at school and it is making us ill. My friend doesn't even come to school anymore. We are frightened of making mistakes. Why are we frightened of making mistakes?' Adam, aged fourteen

○ **They want us to help them develop the skills they need to take their own lives forward.** 'We often find the way you plan our lives means we struggle to plan our own once you have finished. We want to develop our own ability to solve problems and see the bigger picture.' Vicky, aged nineteen

○ **They want to explore their ability to create new things without feeling embarrassed about making mistakes.** 'I was born creative and interested in loads of stuff outside of school, but I feel embarrassed when I tell you what I really care about.' Amy, aged sixteen

○ **They don't like conflict but sometimes feel it is the only way to get you to stop and listen.** 'You make it about "them and us" because you don't stop and listen!' André, aged seventeen

○ **They think that we are too insecure to believe in them.** 'You are frightened to trust us and believe in us and that hurts.' Joe, aged fifteen

These comments should come as no surprise, but thankfully, many young people are thriving despite the challenges they face. You may be at the centre of some of the wonderful work going on around the world and it is incredibly encouraging. But should mainstream society expect more from young people?

Let's do a thought experiment. Imagine you're a science teacher working in a school and I approach you to talk about two new students.

Sally has a gift for chemistry. She spends a lot of time outside of school attending chemistry-related events, visiting science labs, and writing about Nobel Prize winners who have inspired her. She would be an asset to your class and would fit in easily.

Jack is full of potential. His academic record suggests he should be in your class, but he has a poor work ethic. He likes to coast but won't be any trouble.

A whole raft of research points to the likelihood that you would focus your attention on Sally. You would see her excel beyond what Jack would achieve. But what I haven't told you is that Jack and Sally have maintained the same academic profile and level of results throughout their time in school. The research shows that when we have higher expectations of someone and give this person quality time, they achieve much more.

Young people will always tell us that society underestimates them. But by expecting more we can have a profound effect on their lives. If we choose to reach beyond what we think we see in them, then we give young people a stage on which they can perform and reach their potential.

Ever tried it? Inspiring them to raise their game and reach for something bigger and better is exciting. If we expect more they'll deliver. Give them the chance. Their future might just depend on it.

So, what happened to David? I spent some time with him and his family. I considered all my contacts, found a grassroots training provider with the creativity and flare to see his value, and arranged for him to get involved. Sadly, things didn't work out, and I often drive past his house and wonder about him. Should I go back? Should I not take no for an answer? I always hope our heartfelt discussions left some form of legacy, and that he and his family will find a way forward.

David is a victim of a system that leaves huge gaps for young people to fall into. We'll explore this next.

CHAPTER TWO

Mind The Gap

Are you frustrated with bureaucracy? Or annoyed with how disconnected things seem to be? Our systems are not finely tuned machines, and this presents a real worry when it comes to young people.

Mainstream society loves to organise our education, health and social care systems into neat rows and put them into flow charts that look impressive on paper but fail to reflect changes in the real world. But we are human beings after all, with egos and opinions that can thwart our valiant attempts to make the kind of impact we need to make. We spend more time designing and maintaining our systems than we do connecting with the young people they are designed to support.

We design education, healthcare, and social care systems that possess a fundamental flaw. They struggle to communicate with one another. Don't get me wrong: they do talk to each other, but they don't actually communicate, not in a way that means they develop a shared understanding of the young person's real story. Each owns only part of the story. And we know that compartmentalised viewpoints are dangerous.

I've been in meetings where mainstream professionals from the health, social care and education fields all look warily at each other, as a young person's story is described. Each professional is there for a reason but despite good intentions, little progress is made. It's because no one tends to take responsibility. It is the same the world over. It means that youth organisations, charities, social groups, and individuals are picking up the pieces because mainstream professionals struggle to communicate and connect with each other in a meaningful way.

Our world is highly connected. We see globalisation and rapid technological change. Ideas spread easily, regardless of the value they hold, and we feel the impact of fluctuating financial markets on our global banking systems. Like a stone thrown into a pond, the slightest change ripples through our global society.

But the irony is that our lives are *fragmented*. People fail to connect or communicate even when other people's lives depend on it. We live in social 'hubs' and distance ourselves from others. Ever tried telling a joke to a crowded train? I did once. We shouldn't be fooled by connections that look sound on the surface but are only skin deep.

We are human beings and we need to connect on a personal level. We need to think more deeply about how we interact. Gaps appear when communication is merely superficial. We fail to listen to those calling out for our help. Systems that work well on paper never work as well in real life because human relationships are more fluid and reactive. So doesn't it make sense to factor this in when we design them?

Did you know our systems have blind spots?

Blind spots are extremely dangerous. I joke with my family that my eighty-year-old father-in-law hasn't had a car accident for twenty years but many people who've encountered him have. Ignorance isn't bliss: it's dangerous. (His driving isn't that bad, so don't worry.)

When we design systems of support or work within them, we carry a huge responsibility. Not only are our systems not perfect (not that hard to see), but also, the things they miss by design can have a catastrophic effect. We need to recognise this.

For example, let's consider job descriptions and boundaries. Imagine a young person enjoying themselves on a surfboard on a sunny day. Then the tide takes them away from shore. They're struggling to get back, and the alarm has been raised. You've been sent out to rescue them.

As you approach, you reach out and lift them into the boat. But before you return to the safety of the shore, you check to see if they fit into the specifications of your job role. You let them know how concerned you are about the distressing position they find themselves in, but as you delve a little deeper, you realise they don't quite fit the profile of the type of person you would normally be commissioned to save. They look both annoyed and concerned and ask what will happen next. You tell them they'll have to get out again and wait. You tell them how sorry you are but that someone else should be along to get them, if they can keep afloat until then.

Stupid as it sounds, this is what often happens to young people asking for help from mainstream services. Often, no one comes at all. We would be naive to think there aren't any gaps. We continue to assume that society, having made so many mistakes in the past, has it sorted now. But highly skilled and capable individuals feel unable to move forward because of the curse of our professional boundaries.

Short-term thinking versus long-term thinking

Not surprisingly, we think short term most of the time. Once we start working in small, discrete teams and within strict professional boundaries, we put up walls around ourselves and disconnect from other teams. It's not necessarily wrong to specialise. There are times when certain skills are needed – but not at the expense of connection. Young people fall through these communication gaps, and we rarely notice.

Short-term thinking also affects the way we plan and organise our support. It can cause us to become risk averse. And focusing on what is immediate can also reduce the depth of our thinking. I hope you agree with me when I say that young people's lives are a long-term investment.

Do you find yourself trapped within your job role, and strict criteria? Often we're conflicted when we see a young person's well-being slipping through our fingers because we can't leave the confines of our job role.

Short-term thinking on its own can be detrimental to both young people (as it impacts on their ability to think long-term and make plans) and those working with them. It doesn't allow you to think about the bigger picture and work towards a brighter future, beyond the immediate crisis that might be unfolding. The support we offer should liberate them and not hold them back. But if short-term goals are seen just as a means to an end, we have the chance to help young people create a more sustainable future for themselves and one that plays to their strengths.

Most of us who work with young people see our work as a vocation rather than a job. A job is about the short term – it's about the job description and passing the young people on to the next stage. But we should all be concerned about what happens to them next. If your work is a vocation, you will feel concern about the state of things and will want to make your mark.

I was once called to an important meeting with a student, her mum, and the school. Things weren't going well for the student, and it took a colleague's reaching outside of her own professional boundaries to connect me with this case. Otherwise, my involvement wouldn't have happened.

They explained the situation to me: they were planning their seventh attempt to get her back into school. She was highly anxious, and not coping. Things had been so bad that the last time she was in school, she was literally banging her head against a wall to try to block out the emotional pain.

During the meeting, I asked a direct question, and I still remember it after all these years. 'Can you imagine inviting her into the school office and then grabbing her by the hair and banging her head into the wall?' Of course, the answer was no. But it made the teachers stop and think about the way they were dealing with this remarkable young lady. I encouraged them to think and act differently.

When systems don't communicate we all feel like banging our heads against brick walls. If we don't look beyond our specialisms and try to connect with those whose ideas and practices can help us find better solutions, we'll carry on making the same mistakes.

As you travel through these pages, you will learn how the Sixty-day Challenge, along with your own desire for change, can begin to make things better.

We are all part of a continuous cycle of change. Behind the scenes, complex social and economic factors force mainstream society to reconsider its aims and objectives regularly. And young people's lives are deeply affected by these shifts in social thinking.

Does mainstream society ever learn from its mistakes? The simple answer is rarely. Those who have spent decades within education, health and social care systems see the same mistakes happen again and again, and the same 'solutions' surface. Mainstream society thinks it's innovating but doesn't realise it has tried these things before.

The role of youth organisations around the world should be to provide innovative and well-designed solutions to the problems society faces. If we understand why gaps appear and what it takes to bridge them, we'll be well placed to do so. And there's something that sets those who do this apart from the mainstream.

CHAPTER THREE

The Lost Sheep Principle

In 2007 Sergio Fajardo, the son of one of Colombia's most famous architects, became mayor of Medellin. The city had long been regarded as one of the most dangerous cities in the world. The rich and the powerful sit within guarded boundaries while the poor live in the foothills, separated both physically and socially.

These slums, known as *favelas*, have been a battleground, where local drug barons and government forces fight a vicious war. Innocent children and young people trapped inside this environment suffer on a large scale.

Fajardo had a simple but audacious idea. He would connect the favelas to the rest of the city by redirecting the city's resources. He built a modern transit system that enables workers from the favelas to travel into the city. He also invested in building cutting-edge public buildings (libraries, schools and social centres) throughout the favelas.

Though the situation in Medellin is still far from idyllic, what Fajardo did was rare. He looked out at the periphery of the city. He saw the marginalised and decided it was no longer acceptable for the city to ignore them.

Fajardo was living and working by the Lost Sheep Principle.

For most of us, mainstream society provides a haven. We live our lives in relative anonymity, and rarely come across the kinds of problems we occasionally hear about on the news.

But mainstream thinking has a fundamental flaw – it generalises. It plies its trade in the law of averages. It uses statistics to measure and define itself, and those on the fringes are often statistically irrelevant. Many struggle to keep up with mainstream thinking and go missing. They fall behind and get lost, but because they are on the periphery of our vision, we don't see it happening, or connect with the consequences.

The Lost Sheep Principle (LSP) represents a standard, a moral code, and reveals the behaviour of a social ecosystem that averts its gaze from those wandering on the periphery of society, alone and vulnerable. If you're working with vulnerable young people, you will identify with LSP.

It's not that mainstream society doesn't care about the lost and vulnerable, but there are times when it becomes trapped in its thinking. Groupthink has particularly damaging effects.

Living and working by mainstream thinking	Living and working by the Lost Sheep Principle
You accept generalisations	You want to specialise
You focus on the conventional	You think in unconventional ways
You move forward without reflecting	You stop and listen and then reflect
You operate within defined social boundaries	You want to break free of social boundaries
You have access to most resources	You struggle to gain access to resources
You use labels easily and like them	You see beyond labels
You focus on the majority	You focus on individuals and small groups
You're happy with a one-size-fits-all solution	You want to develop bespoke solutions
You have a short attention span regarding social issues	You retain focus on social issues over the longer term
You don't see what's happening on the periphery of society	You focus on what's happening on the periphery of society
You assume that collateral damage is inevitable	You find the concept of collateral damage highly unacceptable
You have clear opportunities to voice your opinions but rarely feel a need to	You find it hard to get your voice heard
What you do for a living is just a job	What you do for a living is a vocation
It's unlikely you help the lost to find their voices	You want to help the lost tell their stories
It's unlikely you encounter the vulnerable, and if you do, it's unlikely you will be able to connect with them	You fight to connect with the vulnerable and most likely succeed
You are risk averse	Risk is inherent in what you do

In high-pressure group situations, individuals can lose their ability to think outside of themselves. If they have powerful decisions to make, we should be worried. Groups trapped in this way will be unable to listen to other viewpoints and will take what they feel is the moral high ground.

No one should be making careless decisions when young people's lives are at stake, but on occasion, powerful groups don't listen. They make mistakes. Rash decisions are often the signature of groupthink. Thankfully, circumstances rarely align in this way.

The last few years have been challenging in the UK. We have suffered awful attacks on our liberty that have affected us deeply. We have also become powerfully aware of how young people all around the world are being exploited and mistreated.

Such events present us with windows of opportunity. A light comes on. It's bright enough to illuminate the dark places of mainstream thinking, if only for a time. These moments of clarity see mainstream thinking and the LSP join forces. The lost find their voice, albeit for a fleeting moment – but real change is possible. Later, we'll look at how we can take advantage of windows of opportunity in real, practical ways.

Living in mainstream society requires certain attributes – without them, young people can quickly find themselves on the fringes of society.

- They need access to a good support network. This might include a supportive family with the capacity to raise their aspirations and provide some financial support, too. Good relationships with adults outside of the family are also important. If they don't have these relationships, we'll often lose sight of them.

- They need to develop their resilience as they navigate through mainstream society. They need to develop the strength of character to hold their ground in the storms that batter us all emotionally. Without this, young people can crash emotionally. Robust mental health is important, too.

- They need to be able to compromise. Our systems can be quite unforgiving. Most of the 'compromising' is done by the young people themselves because the systems are uncompromising. Sometimes this is too difficult for the young to manage and they fall away.

- They need to have a strong understanding of how relationships work, and a strong grasp of social rules and expectations. Society carries a lot of unwritten rules. If you understand them, great. If you don't, you'll have problems. It's not easy living in the world today, and falling away and becoming lost isn't as difficult as we might think.

Sadly, we live in an imperfect world, and it's worrying that there are people who manage to exploit the gaps. We know there are those who hide in dark places. They are skilled at flattering the unwary and leading them astray with empty promises. And they often hide in plain sight.

In 2011, terrible news was brought to the surface in Manchester, UK. A group of men was charged with the systematic abuse of teenage girls. The agencies charged with keeping these girls safe had been failing them for a long time. Everything was brushed under the carpet.

The girls had to be extremely brave amid a staggering lack of empathy from many professionals. They were blamed for their own circumstances.

It took a 'tribe' of professionals working together to connect with the girls and their families at a much deeper level and bridge the gap between them and the systems they had to navigate to tell their stories. This book aims to promote the development of these tribes. Unfortunately, as those who are familiar with this story will tell you, standing up for the lost doesn't always go well.

In the UK, as in many countries, social agendas come and go. Many are designed to keep us accountable, to ensure that all children and young people are cared for.

Once again, these agendas may look great on paper, but translating them into real life and developing the connections necessary to make everything work is another story.

The LSP speaks about the need to meet the young person wherever they are. It embodies a way of living and working that creates champions happy to take risks and challenge the status quo. We must think carefully about how bridges are built and how mainstream society's indifference can be used as a catalyst for change.

And yes, every child does matter.

The relationships we build are central to how we start unlocking their potential.

CHAPTER FOUR

Learning Relationships

Many years ago, I was a soldier (those who know me now find this hard to imagine!). It was physically demanding at times. Once basic training was over, I studied aircraft engineering, and worked on helicopter engines. I only lasted about three years in the army – just long enough to say I gave it a go.

The army is the kind of place where clear hierarchical structures are important. You can't go into battle challenging the commands handed down through the ranks. Popping by the command tent to ask 'Do you really think it's a good idea to attack the gun emplacement at dawn' isn't likely to go down well.

Soldiering wasn't for me. What does the army do with soldiers who want to challenge their thinking? They made my leaving easy.

It has been a real privilege working with young people over the past thirty years. I've spent time working in youth centres. I've also worked with young people in their homes (some can't leave their houses because of crippling anxiety). I've work in schools, in classes, and have been a careers adviser. At times I've been responsible for small teams. And throughout my countless one-to-one conversations with young people (some planned, others spur of the moment), I've come to believe in the win-win scenario.

I suspect you find it fulfilling when your relationships with young people are highly productive – when *your* objectives (perhaps you're a teacher with tight deadlines or a social worker looking to secure a new placement) are successfully met. You connect well with the young person, gain their trust, find innovate solutions, and make real progress. But the relationship will work much better when you respect *their* values, wants, and needs, when you find common ground and shared objectives and know deep down that the relationship you've developed meets both your needs.

Learning relationships work quite differently compared to the top-down approach of hierarchical relationships.

It's frustrating to see how often young people are isolated. Don't get me wrong, I know there are times when young people need to be challenged and authority needs to be exercised, but if this is your only approach, you're on rocky ground.

The win-win scenario isn't about being soft. It's about being firm (when required) but fair. It's about respect and the desire to learn from our mistakes and share responsibility. The hierarchical approach is focused solely on the 'I-win' scenario rather than on the 'we-can-all-win' scenario. This top-down approach is one dimensional and often guilty of causing harm. Let me explain.

As someone who works with young people, what are your objectives? What are you trying to achieve? Whenever I ask this question, the answers vary immensely.

They might include 'I want the student to gain a qualification', or 'I want to help them find a work placement'. Then I press further and ask: 'What about the young person?' Then people get it. They start thinking more long-term and about how they can help develop in the young person the kinds of skills they need to have a successful life. They talk about the young person's strengths and passions. They wonder how they can inspire them to think more creatively beyond the immediate. These are the reasons most of us start working with young people in the first place, and a purely top-down approach cannot achieve these goals.

Hierarchical relationships, particularly those that are multi-layered, have their problems.

- ✪ Those at the bottom of the hierarchy (generally young people) often feel isolated.

- ✪ Misunderstandings are common and often difficult to put right.

- ✪ There is little genuine communication, and it certainly isn't two way.

- ✪ When it matters the most, loyalty is not given.

- Power struggles or internal fighting and rebellion are more likely.

- Feedback is generic and lacks focus. The truth is rarely discussed.

- Trust is easily broken because the connections are highly fragile.

- They provide a breeding ground for a 'them and us' mentality.

If you've worked in large organisations that don't really involve everyone in their development, particularly in terms of values and mission, then you know the impact this has on individuals. Large (and brave) structural change is required to help everyone feel valued and part of the processes.

We wrongly assume that adults and those in power always know better, but the reality is that we often don't. We keep on making the same mistakes. We need to open our minds to the possibility that young people possess a real capacity to work in harness with us to make the best of the systems we're all engaged in.

It seems many people assume that the stick-and-carrot approach to punishment and reward works all the time – but it doesn't. I choose not to drive while using my mobile phone because I worry someone might get hurt or die through my stupidity. The thought of getting a fine and points on my licence only provides extra weight.

We do need laws and we do need rules. We also need to see them used consistently. But the point I'm making is that most of us are motivated intrinsically, and young people are no different.

Control relies on the systematic use of these motivational tools. But it only destabilises. Like everyone else in the world, young people look for autonomy. They look for the opportunity to develop their social skills and their ability to manage themselves. They need help setting their own boundaries. Autonomy has a powerful effect on their performance and their attitude. With autonomy, they start caring and they start believing in better.

Young people don't want to be like pawns on a chessboard, moved around by someone else. They want to be players.

Whenever I speak to colleagues about this I hear the same kinds of concerns. They say that young people cannot be trusted because they don't have the skills to take responsibility. To this, I respond that hierarchical thinking actually deskills young people. It becomes a self-fulfilling prophesy. On the other hand, learning relationships can help develop these skills.

In the same vein, people say that the systems will collapse if we give young people more autonomy. Hierarchical systems are fragile. They rely on control, rule, fear, and punishment to keep everyone in line. This fear permeates our systems. These systems are prone to collapse. It is the strength and number of learning relationships happening that can tip the balance.

Some people tell me that young people don't care. Some are past caring. We shouldn't blame them for this. We should look at ourselves. I'm never happy when a young person punches a wall or a teacher, when they bully or when they get high on drugs. But if we don't know what's going on in their lives and only care about the immediate, job-specific goals, how can we be surprised? If you treated me like that I would withdraw and struggle to see the point in conforming.

People tell me that they don't have the time to develop these deeper relationships. But learning relationships aren't about how much time you have but about how you choose to connect when you get the chance. It's amazing what you can achieve in brief moments. Successful interactions build momentum.

Unfortunately, most of us still think in hierarchical terms. We haven't truly grasped the full power and explosive potential of learning relationships. We should.

At the heart of the learning relationship is the decision to connect. It's not a relationship that makes you feel vulnerable. It can be a means to an end, but it's never one-sided. Both individuals learn from the experience.

I tell young people that we are all human beings trying to make the best of the opportunities we have, so we should agree to help each other. Here are some key attributes of the learning relationship.

Shared values

I have my own values. I've learned to understand them and articulate them. They matter to me and I won't sit by and let them be trampled on. But when talking to a young person, what I try hard to show them is that I'm choosing to respect and learn about *their* values, about what matters to *them*.

I often find young people rarely stop and think about their values, but it is a delight when youth organisations help them to do this. If both parties gain a clear understanding of each other's values, shared values can emerge, and the connection made will be stronger.

Clear roles and responsibilities

Any relationship with a young person outside of your own family requires clear terms and conditions. It's a transaction, but one between human beings on a level playing field who want the best for each other.

I will always make my role clear. I'll tell the young person what I'm there for and what responsibilities I have. I will then tell them about their responsibilities. I'm often startled by what motivates a young person and how they perceive my motivations. It's fundamental to gain a shared understanding of motivations. This will help to prevent confusion later, and ensure a reliable forum for feedback.

High expectations

I want to inspire young people to reach for their best. Nothing about the way I talk to them suggests less. Learning relationships cause us to believe in young people and to encourage them to reach higher than they might have thought possible.

Trust

Do young people trust you? Do you trust them? Will you honour your commitments? Do they think you will? Building trust takes time, but it's always worth the effort. With trust, you're in a position to experiment and make mistakes. Working together, you can take calculated risks and learn to solve problems more effectively. And if young people trust you, they will tell others about you – in an organisation such as a school, this kind of reputation is important.

Helping young people see the benefit of relationships is important. It's also important they recognise that the playing field is level and they have a great deal to offer. It's down to us to ensure they recognise this and learn to exploit it.

While learning relationships offer a wonderful opportunity to bring about meaningful change in the lives of young people, they can also offer a foundation for something longer lasting. I call it the Rule of Threes.

The Rule of Threes encourages you to see beyond the immediate, to make the relationship three-way. It's about putting young people in contact with other people who can help them move forward and access new opportunities. You act as a broker, always looking for ways to extend their horizons. As adults, we're responsible for the quality of the relationship and accountable for where it leads. Can mainstream organisations think this way?

Mainstream society rarely strays from the confines of the hierarchical approach, but learning relationships happen within them all the time. They are the glue in the systems. They pick up the pieces of broken and ineffective systems, drawing people and objectives together. They are rarely centre stage.

As we'll discuss in Part Two, learning relationships can benefit greatly from our ability to tell stories – both our own and others'.

PART TWO

Making Connections

CHAPTER FIVE

Using Our Stories To Unlock Theirs

I'm rather fond of a good story. Stephen King is one of my favourites (the traditionalists among you may be surprised). In fact, I don't think I've ever met anyone who doesn't like to hear a good story or, if given the chance, to tell one. But why?

Stories cross boundaries. Stories travel across space and time. They need no entry visa and they don't restrict themselves to particular social groups – they take on all comers. We can all share stories passed down the ages, and many carry important moral messages and truths that resonate deeply with us.

Stories can act as 'currency'. All over the world, people barter using stories. For generations, travellers have earned a meal and bed for the night on the strength of their ability to share stories of their adventures.

Storytelling requires no special qualifications. You need only to be human and have the desire to connect with someone. Even if you can't speak, you can tell a story. They are easy to share.

Stories help us sell ourselves. Anyone who has to persuade others for a living can use stories to present their values or mission.

Stories offer multiple points of contact. A story can appeal to a range of emotions, and affect people in often unexpected ways. We sometimes tell stories as if we think they are lasers, focusing on a particular point, but someone can highlight how it has impacted them in a remarkably different way than intended.

Stories connect us. Stories bring people together more effectively than any other medium. They help us find common ground and reveal shared values. They open up conversations, help soothe broken hearts, and help us understand ourselves better.

Fictional stories can do this. But real-life stories connect us to each other more deeply than any fictional character or plot ever could.

Many years ago, at a church meeting, someone I'd known for a number of years stood up and shared something that had a huge impact on me. She described how for the past ten years, she'd been drinking heavily at home. She'd hidden it from her family and her friends but had begun feeling drawn to come to terms with it and make changes. It was a powerful testimony.

Someone once said that there's a book in all of us. I don't agree with or deny this. But what I do think is that we all have a story to tell – and every story can be powerful.

This book is about how to find common ground with young people, understand their perspective, and find innovative ways to create lasting and effective change. The people I've met who manage this on a regular basis always tap into their own stories and experiences. It requires bravery and, for some, a real shift in their thinking.

Your story is powerful. It is powerful in the telling. It is powerful in the sharing. It is powerful because it is real.

I have already shared how, at school, I was highly anxious and had problems getting my words out. This issue continued affecting me into my twenties, even when I was in the army. I'd always been a deep thinker, so I looked for a way out of the maze. After a good deal of heartache, I finally stumbled into the daylight determined to turn the difficulties into something good.

Often, times of great hardship bring out things in us that are worth sharing. But it's the collection of every experience, both good and bad, that helps us form our stories.

What power does your story hold? What brought you here to read this book? Are you driven by strong feelings of injustice? Did you struggle as a child? Do you struggle on the fringes of society with the lost sheep? Do you have a growing desire to make an impact on their lives?

Earlier I quoted Mark Twain and his maxim to the effect that the two greatest days in our lives are the day we are born and the day we find out why. Don't underestimate the power your story holds – it's your 'why' that provides you with the strength to carry on when things get hard. If you don't feel a connection with your own story, you just end up going through the motions. Young people need to connect with people who value the fact that they are living their lives right now, just like you are. As you begin to unlock the power within your own story and learn to share it with others, amazing things can happen.

- ◔ Young people begin to see how the choices they make impact on their futures but that nothing is set in stone

- ◔ They learn that being vulnerable is normal

- ◔ They start to see the value in their own stories

- ◔ They begin to realise they are capable of far more than they first realised (you can show them the value hidden within life's struggles)

- ◔ They learn that complex social problems can be solved by connecting with others through their own stories

Youth organisations all around the world need to tap into their stories. Larger organisations can find this difficult. As tribes expand and become more organised and professional, they may lose sight of why they started in the first place. We all need to connect with each other and develop learning relationships so the young people who rely on us can share their journeys.

How you tell your story and what you share is of course down to you. You don't have to talk about the personal stuff. Just remember that our stories are bigger than we are. They are entwined in other people's lives: the people we meet, the people we love, and the people we don't. The stories I tell are often about how my relationships with others have changed the way I think. I talk about the lessons I've learned. Essentially, I share how my life has intersected with other people's lives and how this affected me.

There is much more to each of us than we let people see. Our privacy matters – there are things we just don't want others to know and that's fine. But there's still so much we can share. I generally ask myself: 'If this thing that I'm sharing with one person got out to everyone else, would I mind?' If the answer is no, I feel comfortable sharing it.

I share stories about my previous jobs (eg, about my time in the army, or teaching tennis in the United States). I also talk about what it was like being unemployed and stuck in my room. I speak about my travels, and tell stories about nearly dead hamsters and hiding from my sergeant major as he did his inspection. Young people need to see you are a human being, and not just someone doing a job. If they feel they are just a 'number', you will not connect with them.

Good storytellers do the following:

- build suspense and use humour. Of course we aren't all stand-up comedians, but there's nothing more effective in breaking down barriers than humour. I even do impressions (clearly these aren't compulsory)

- keep it simple: watch out for eyes glazing over or stifled yawns

- display passion: there's always time for a little emotion. Don't start crying on their shoulder, but remember that young people value a little vulnerability at the right time, and your vulnerability will make them more likely to come back and see you again

- aren't afraid of uncomfortable silences. I like to sit and say nothing sometimes. (Not for too long, but I do set the scene and tell them I'm thinking.)

- tell the truth

- aren't afraid to make simple statements

When you begin to think seriously about your own story, about the things that make you happy and the things that drive you crazy, you start to see the wealth of experience that you have – experience that provides an opportunity for young people to learn about themselves and the world around them. Someone once described those adept at connecting well with young people as lighthouses.

The comparison is a little corny, but if we can stop young people from crashing onto the rocks by shining our light in their general direction, then surely making the effort is worthwhile.

Your story is powerful. Stop and reflect on it and you might just surprise yourself.

So, armed with a greater desire to connect through the power of stories, how do we go on to meet young people face to face, and what might our objectives be?

CHAPTER SIX

Unlocking Potential, One Life At A Time

All youth organisations are driven by the desire to see young people's lives change for the better, but what do we really want to see happening in their lives?

I often think deeply about this. When I see reports outlining some of the awful human rights abuses across the globe (and I know many of you are actively involved in addressing this instead of writing a book), I reframe the question. I ask, 'What do I no longer want to see?'

I don't want to see young people waking up in the morning fearful for their safety. I don't want them to be abused. I don't want mainstream society to be blind to the gaps that young people can fall through.

I do want to see a world where people like you and me change mainstream thinking, where the brilliant work of so many youth organisations gains even greater focus and power. For this to happen, we need to listen, and to listen, we need to stop.

Young people's stories are often spoken in a whisper. In a noisy world, we often miss them. They can also be hard to decipher amid opinions and assumptions. Mainstream society struggles to connect on a personal level. But it is here, face to face, where it all begins. Here, we gain the kind of understanding that will prepare us for the challenge of creating lasting change.

Importantly, this is something we can all get better at. I often thank young people for helping me to refine my views. Though I set out to inspire and equip them, they also inspire and equip me. The process of sharing brings out the best in everyone. It reveals the power of the learning relationship.

The twelve keys to unlocking potential

Having spent many years listening to young people and helping them learn to solve their own social problems, I've picked out these twelve 'keys' to unlocking potential. Many of them are found in the mission statements of organisations that work with young people.

1. Help them discover where their strengths lie and how they can exploit them. Generic systems, the kind that our young people find themselves in, measure success and failure in generic terms. Our education systems present a key example. It's important to have a good grounding in maths and language, but so many amazing young people leave school with little idea of what they're good at and where their passions lie. This is a travesty. I ask young people what they do when they aren't at school.

Some speak with great passion about their ideas, skills, and interests. I help them develop these. Others look at me rather shocked: 'What do you mean?' Such passion hasn't yet been explored. Sometimes you need to prise it out with a crowbar! But once you light a fire like this, it's not easily extinguished.

A by-product of this approach is the young person's realisation that every learning opportunity can be used as a means to an end. It can guide them towards a more positive outcome. They are good at something! And it matters! They can start seeing themselves as an individual with a voice. This is the kind of potential we want to unlock.

2. Help them to think more deeply about the questions they ask, instead of judging them on their answers to your questions. Young people often try to give us the answers they think we want to hear. But we should see past generic answers to generic questions because that's where their stories really lie. Challenge them to think about their environments: home, school, community. Encourage them to think more deeply about where their path might lead and what control they have over their current path. Let's show them how to ask effective questions and how to get the feedback they need from those around them. When you think about the kind of change you want to see, your questions change.

Should we show them how to be assertive? This means teaching them how to come to terms with their own values, but also how to compromise and respect other people's values. Without the ability to ask the right questions, how can they do so?

3. Spend more time showing them productive ways of thinking, instead of what to think. There are a great many anxious children in the world. Many assume their abilities and capacity for growth are predetermined. We all need to continually challenge our grasp of what is real and true. Often, strong emotions take us for a ride, and we see our experiences through an emotional lens. Too many young people wake up in the morning with negative expectations – and they don't know why. It is amazing to see young people begin to use different terminology and challenge their own assumptions. And when these assumptions are challenged, minds become more agile and doors open.

I love to work on mindsets, particularly on fixed and growth mindsets. We should work hard to help young people see that intelligence isn't fixed and that they can achieve amazing things with the right focus and some hard work. They can learn that their thinking isn't fixed, either. I say, 'Why not think positively in the morning?' We should help them to explore other thinking options.

4. Consider the academic, emotional, social, and creative challenges they face. How young people face challenges is as important as the challenges themselves. I'm keen to help them think about ways to do so. Some challenges are forced upon them through circumstance, and can really hurt (eg, family breakdown, death of a loved one, loss of a home, ill health). It's important they feel supported and can see the bigger picture.

Learning opportunities should reflect the full range of experience. We should try to bring people together to share ideas and insights. It enriches their understanding and helps them see they aren't alone if things get tough. It also expands their horizons. I like to show them ways they can solve their own social problems and ask for help when they need it.

5. Show them how to take a more active role in their community. I strongly believe that communities should play an active role in helping young people develop their skills and wisdom. Communities are often fragmented, but you can find groups keen to support. Young people often choose to avoid more organised groups, distrusting their intentions. We should encourage them to grow to appreciate the potential their communities hold and take calculated risks. I have often taken young people into theatres or galleries, or introduced them to artisan workers who help them see beyond their immediate environment. They start to explore new skills and opportunities.

I also believe in the power of giving. Joy and satisfaction are found in sharing what you know or helping someone else. Young people can appear selfish, but if they grow up with a greater appreciation of what it feels like to help others then all the better. If they learn to be assertive while still being open to sharing their lives with others, they can lead more fulfilling lives.

We should also encourage them to empathise. I don't ask them to sympathise with people and their causes, because sympathy doesn't allow for the kind of deep connection that really makes a difference. Empathy makes them more creative, and better at solving problems. The more empathy we all show, the better things work.

6. Help them to think more globally about learning. There are many learning opportunities outside of school, so I try to help them unpack the diversity of these opportunities. Some young people, due to their unique perspectives on life, think they need permission to think creatively. For reasons that are often complex, learning in mainstream settings can present challenges. But we should challenge young people to see beyond the conventional whatever their situation. Where do learning opportunities present themselves? How do these opportunities look? How can the young person explore what is available? What do they want to try out?

7. Help them see the value in accessing other people's wisdom and experience, and encourage them to share their own insights. As discussed earlier, learning relationships are two-way. We all need to see the good in others, and how their stories can help us grow. Have you ever disliked someone and believed the feeling was mutual? I have – only to find out years later that we have some shared values, and misread each other in the past. We all possess insight; we just need to be open to seeing it in others. Learning relationships demand a growing mutual respect. Get past the ego, fear, and strong opinions and you can get far more out of every interaction.

8. Encourage them to explore the world around them and see it as a stepping stone towards understanding themselves better. It can be difficult to see past your immediate environment. Those who can do this tend to see potential and opportunity when others might not. Too many young people are trapped by the thinking of people close to them who fail to see the power in exploring the world. Our immediate environments and the thinking that comes from them often fail to illuminate the riches beyond. In the UK, we are fond of saying 'the grass isn't always greener on the other side'. We shouldn't look down our noses at the wisdom and freedom present in our immediate environment. But we shouldn't be afraid to explore. I find this idea is often a new one to the young people I work with. Let's always look to expand their horizons.

9. Help them find opportunities to collaborate with others. Collaboration is important. But the way we go about it is often generic – we put young people in groups and judge them on their contribution. It's naive to hold rigid views about how to be part of a discussion.

All young people have a great deal to contribute towards

each other's and our lives. But should an anxious child be expected to stand up and speak in class? Should the introvert have to shout? Each person has their own key to unlocking their own potential, and it's our job to help them find it and use it. When we consider that our views are often ill-informed and sometimes made in haste, we can begin to slow down and start watching. Expanding our ability to help others contribute results in a win-win scenario. We should ask young people how they like to share their ideas and solutions, and the barriers to their doing this. It's amazing what you can uncover.

10. Help them to see mistakes as important learning tools. Why are so many young people afraid to make mistakes? Many carry a strong fear of rejection. They take things immensely personally. But when they gain a more constructive view of rejection, their lives can be transformed. I see fear leave them. I see them become unafraid of the word 'no'. I try to show them that rejection is rarely about them, and more about the other person or system – that it's often a matter of opinion.

A huge amount of work is done around the world on the growth mindset. I meet too many young people with fixed mindsets. They are afraid to consider they can improve their lot in life. When rejection is viewed as a learning opportunity, mindsets completely change.

11. Encourage them to keep trying, to never lose hope, and to take responsibility for their own futures. Are young people merely reacting to their environments and thinking short term? For many, especially those whose family lives are inconsistent, it's a real challenge to think long-term. Survival is their priority. Many young people experience awful things, but those who show the most promise are those who refuse to lose hope. We should encourage them to reflect on what they do have, and how they can build on that. I talk to them about dreams and why we have them. I can't pick them up out of their current situations – they are often fighting against their histories, current environments, and culture– but there is always a way forward. They can start to believe there is a better way.

12. Encourage them to appreciate the knowledge and wisdom of ages past. There is much to be gained from exploring our collective past. But if young people deeply distrust our often-fragmented world, they are unlikely to see the lessons that can be learned from past mistakes. We can tell them about how people all around the world respond to problems, and act in different ways. I quote the wise and insightful and try to show them how other people's stories carry a wealth of opportunity for personal growth. We shouldn't be afraid to share something of our own journeys, either.

What these keys reveal is the need for us to see the bigger picture. Youth organisations are often driven by their own objectives, and struggle to be holistic. There is little doubt that your objectives are important and well thought out, but you still need to be open to considering what else might be going on. We need to approach each interaction with a young person, whatever our role, without a rigid agenda.

Whenever we meet with a young person, it's important to be honest. It's also important to model the kind of attitude we're asking them to develop. We should meet them with an agile mind, one that's open to hearing their stories and able to draw from previous experiences.

I'm strict on the fact that it's not my goal to 'fix' them. The problem is rarely just about them – there's usually much more happening under the surface. I often find young people just want some reassurance. It makes a big difference when they realise their challenging circumstances are not just down to them.

I believe it's this approach that provides the right foundations to enable young people to succeed and it's not hard to replicate. Strictly speaking, I do have an agenda. I don't turn up to play computer games or learn how to make a quilt – unless these things provide the best way to connect! I turn up to watch and to listen. I need them to quickly see I'm on their side and able to help them navigate a difficult time in their lives.

When I meet with a young person, my 'game plan' forms quickly. I look for points of connection that will help them appreciate that they aren't alone and that someone is willing to see things from their perspective. I balance this out with simple explanations of the systems they find themselves in, and people's motives. I paint a bigger picture and outline their part in it.

As a coach, I then go on to offer an action plan – one with a pace that works for them. Do they want to talk at length for an hour or more? Do they need bite-size sessions so they can process everything? Do they have family and friends they can talk to between our meetings? I once worked with a young man who was a selective mute. We communicated via email twice a week. I asked set questions. This way, he had time to think about his answers.

I always make the effort to get up-to-date feedback from their family and friends, and to find out what terminology the young person uses to describe their situation. I look for the small things. They can result in huge gains. The main point is that we don't know what we'll find, so we need to be open and agile. I find it inspires young people to be the same.

Having no agenda isn't about 'winging it' or being disorganised. Over the past twenty years, I've gained an understanding of the huge array of circumstances a young person can find themselves in. I've organised this information in my head. It's my resource bank, easily accessed when needed. Do you like to read? Do you see patterns? Welcome to my world! It takes a degree of bravery, but if you haven't tried turning up to see a young person with an open mind and blank agenda, then give it a go. You'll be amazed at what you already know and what the young person can teach you.

What if a young person won't speak to you? Get creative. I work with the family, friends and professionals who see them every day, who can support them by proxy, using the same terminology I use. Connecting with young people is about partnership. I share my ideas and strategies. We talk about the touchpoints and what to say to get the information we need.

I've seen large youth organisations that fail to tap in to those workers in their teams who do this. These champions are remarkable – if you can make the most of them, your strategies will be transformed. Did you know that champions also make great detectives?

Sherlock Holmes is a world-famous detective. He isn't real, of course. But his character and methodology provide some interesting talking points. Every youth organisation needs at least one Holmes.

> ○ **He's a master of disguise.** Holmes adopts convincing disguises to infiltrate society and gain the information he needs to solve a case. While I'm not suggesting you wear fancy dress, you can think about how you come across to the young person. For the tough kid, I'm the

ex-soldier, comfortable with banter. For the scared kid, I'm still and calm, prepared to tell a funny story about my journey to put them at ease. I've become a master of disguise and so can you.

◎ **He has a rich and diverse network.** Holmes has a vast support network that enables him to gain information about and insight into even the most obscure problem. We should always work with our networks, and see the skills people have. They may come in handy.

◎ **He has a wide range of interests and vast knowledge.** Holmes consumes knowledge across various fields. He's smart. He does experiments. Though he shows no interest in philosophy, or the mating habits of the lower classes, his knowledge base is always growing. Don't accept the 'expert' tag. Run away from it. Instead, consider wearing a badge that says, 'Still Learning'. When we continue to increase our knowledge, our lives become a more exciting journey.

◎ **He believes there's always an answer, and loves solving complex riddles.** Holmes always thinks that a solution will present itself. If a problem exists, a solution exists. This kind of attitude has profound effects. It means you're open to seeing what's really going on. Young people need us to believe in a solution, even when the circumstances suggest there isn't one. If you do, calmly and with some humour, then they begin to believe, too.

○ **He watches and listens carefully.** Holmes consistently watches and listens. He looks at the details as well as the bigger picture. He knows that small things can have a big impact, and can tilt the scales. He knows that change is inevitable and that the truth will always reveal itself if you're paying attention. Young people don't tell us everything. And they shouldn't have to. If we are to unlock their potential (and develop ways of facilitating this potential and embedding it into mainstream society), we need to keep our ears to the ground.

'Youth detectives' are doing vital work across the globe, but we need to continue thinking outside the box. We need to work with those champions who connect with young people to drive us forward – and we need to listen to them, as they can get to the heart of the matter. If we continue to work in a formulaic way, we will continue to struggle. It takes a special person to adopt a new approach and make it work.

How might we recognise a champion?

CHAPTER SEVEN

The Profile Of A Champion

Young people start their lives putting a great deal of trust in adults. My children are teenagers and they expect me to know the answers to every question they have. I don't. Being a parent unlocks something profound and deep, but whether they have had their own children or not, all champions retain an understanding of what it is to be young.

Young people all over the world need to be supported, advised, and guided through their formative years. Navigating these choppy waters takes a degree of skill and good fortune.

I remember going on a long march during basic training when I was a soldier. It was pitch black. Our platoon sergeant set a remarkable pace. We stumbled. We fell over clumps of grass and lost our footing in holes. The sergeant didn't. He glided. But he was good about it, surprisingly! He later described his own basic training, and how he had done the same. He remembered how it felt.

Young people are on a difficult journey. The more of us with the will and desire to champion their cause, the better. There's something special about the kind of person who has this passion. They might sometimes come across as unreasonable because of their unwavering desire to see things get better. Every young person needs someone to champion their cause. Their lives often depend on it. So we need to know how we can recognise a champion when we see one.

Champions come in all shapes and sizes. They come from all walks of life. They wake up in the morning with the desire to make the world (and the lives of young people) better. They are fully aware of their own fears and insecurities but carry on anyway.

They can be found working in the most inhospitable corners of the globe or in mainstream communities. I meet them in positions of power, trying to change the thinking of large organisations. Sometimes they work alone. Others are in teams. Many are social entrepreneurs. They are found wherever young people struggle. And they are always hoping for the best.

They know how to tap into their own stories and are always open to learning. Many are childlike, full of humour, yet possess a real wisdom that they're always willing to share. They see their work as a vocation, not a job, and if something begins to feel like a job, they're keen to find something new. They are driven by passions. For some, it is a calling.

They are humble and vocal when required. They possess a light that is impossible to extinguish. They shine in the dark places where young people stumble. They are navigators who help young people (and the teams and organisations that support them) to plot a path through difficult terrain.

Are you one of these people?

Let me tell you something else about champions. They often fail to recognise their own value. They don't know how vital they are. Everywhere they go they bring calm and hope. They inspire without even realising it. That's what makes *you* a champion.

Take a look in the mirror. What does it feel like?

Shining a light in the dark places, on the fringes of the mainstream, can be exciting. Champions see the gaps. They see the disconnect and feel its impact keenly – and they take it personally.

We need to be unconventional because convention often doesn't work. It can feel great to be unconventional. But it can also be lonely and frustrating, and that's why those who champion the cause of young people tend to find each other. Conversations are heartfelt and reassuring and partnerships are forged.

Six qualities of a young person's champion

1. An ever-present willingness to keep learning. Champions see opportunities to learn from anyone at any time, especially young people. They know how to develop learning relationships. They reach for challenges and are prepared to make mistakes. They are equally happy to change their plan of action. They think longer term than most, and will not stay loyal to a particular method if it proves ineffective.

2. A desire to share the limelight and work in partnership. Champions rarely care who gets the credit. They are motivated purely by outcomes. They acknowledge the role others have played. They bring people together and give of themselves freely if the young people they are working with will benefit. They look for win-win scenarios.

3. The ability to think outside the box. Champions spend most of their time outside the box. This is because conventional (mainstream) thinking cannot meet their needs. They look to separate themselves from the past and to break free from previously established structures and thinking.

4. A desire to cross boundaries. To make change happen, champions utilise resources and ideas from other fields and domains. They find new connections. They see ways to realign resources. They think about the bigger picture, and they think holistically.

5. A strong moral compass. Champions want young people to fulfil their potential, and to be safe. They want those who want to cause young people harm brought to account. They have a strong sense of right and wrong. They are deeply connected to the idea of social justice and embody the LSP.

6. A willingness to work where few others will. Champions are willing to take risks and work in places and in ways that most people wouldn't. This is because they see their work as a vocation and not a job. Regardless of the personal impact, they step up and take on difficult challenges. They always go the extra mile and keep believing that better is both possible and vital.

Youth organisations operate at their most efficient if they place people like this centre stage and tap into their skills. Champions won't want to be centre stage, but what they have to say and what they see should be. They are your greatest asset.

But being a champion has its challenges. It's never easy championing the cause of young people. Many of us working within large and respected organisations, and with a good reason to challenge mainstream thinking, assume we will be treated well. We often aren't. The mainstream doesn't like its faults being exposed.

Any out-of-the-box thinking can be ridiculed. Only when a truth has been around long enough does it becomes assimilated into the mainstream, as if it were always there. But its journey there is a difficult one.

Have you ever been ignored when you are presenting a solution? The more hard-hitting and direct your approach, the more likely the shock will send the mainstream into a spin and you'll witness childlike behaviour. You'll see large mainstream organisations protecting their own reputations, and you'll see them throwing some big tantrums.

It's all a matter of scale. Are you in a school and pointing out a different approach towards a student? Speak to the right person and things can happen. Are you thinking of going to the press about something huge? Again, speak to the right person. We know there are downsides, but they can be overcome. With that in mind, let's consider some key issues.

Handling mainstream society

Mainstream society often feels swamped by problems. We've already seen how the mainstream can struggle to find solutions. So why not present some potential solutions and offer to put them into action? It's important that we do so in their language. We need to frame solutions clearly and concisely. The mainstream has a complex but restricted vocabulary.

Mainstream society worries about its resources. Organisations may assume you want more of something they don't have enough of! Find ways to show them how you can realign resources, use them more effectively, and create win-win scenarios (which can be found when you look carefully). If they can see you as someone looking to help them do things better, and not looking to increase their workload, they'll be more likely to engage.

Try to find others that you can align with. Working alone is tough (although we've all done it). Try to find people you can align with. Finding your own allies is all part of being a champion as you put the Rule of Threes into action.

Mainstream society doesn't like being shown up, so, keep your anger and passion in check. We need this passion to see that better is possible and that young people are worth investing in, but pick your battles.

It's important to continue getting better at what you do. There's always lots to learn. Here are some ways to develop your profile and skills.

- ◑ **Spend more time with young people**, with the intention of getting better at unlocking their stories. It's amazing what we can learn when they talk about their lives, the way they work things through, and what really matters to them. You'll learn much more about yourself, too.

- ⊙ **Spend more time looking for win-win scenarios.** When your skills in this area improve, life becomes easier. Opportunities will come your way.

- ⊙ **Become more aware of how the mainstream thinks and talks.** Look at how it presents, ignores, and considers its problems, and potential solutions. The greater our understanding of this, the more effective we'll be at finding real solutions.

- ⊙ **Meet with others who think the same way as you do.** It's rewarding to feel validated, and one-to-one conversations with key allies help you hone your thinking.

- ⊙ **Look at different fields and domains to help broaden your skill set.** A knowledge of sociology, business, economics, psychology, theology, and the arts will deepen your understanding of how mainstream society thinks.

- ⊙ **Learn to play to your strengths.** We can all play a role in supporting young people effectively, but we can't all stand up in front of large groups of people, for example. Know your strengths. One-to-one discussions with passion and clear intent can make a real difference.

Teams and organisations need to cultivate the champion mentality. They need to champion young people, and support them in the challenges they face. The difference between teams that do and teams that don't is remarkable. It takes hard work to transform an organisation's culture, but it's important to get it right.

What happens if teams and organisations don't work this way? We know the answer. Gaps appear and young people fall through them. Youth organisations are set up to bridge gaps, not create them. Sometimes mainstream society will recognise its responsibility and pour money into organisations that promise to fill the gaps. But if we lose sight of what we're doing, and the need to champion the cause of young people, then we'll fail, regardless of funding. Teams will stop being teams and become groups of individuals looking out for themselves.

It's not easy running a youth organisation and watching it grow. And those involved with these organisations can face a major dilemma, which we'll look at next.

CHAPTER EIGHT

Staying Or Going?

For many of us, it's a common dilemma: Do we stay on in the teams and organisations with which we currently work? Or do we leave? Do we persevere or pivot? If you have a deep desire to champion the cause of a particular group of young people, you might feel trapped and deskilled in your current setting with little room for manoeuvre. On the other hand, you might be in a position of responsibility with a real opportunity to make a difference, so leaving is not an option.

Change is inevitable. People who have become part of the furniture of an organisation hand in their notices. It often comes as a surprise. What's important in this discussion is whether your environment is capable of supporting you in your desire to use your strengths and passions to make meaningful change in the lives of the young people you support. Can it really respond to your message?

Making the right choice is as much about you as it is about the young people you want to support. Young people need you to be liberated and playing to your strengths so they can be liberated, too.

Our surroundings, including the personalities around us, can have a powerful influence on us. They can often cause us to doubt our motives, and our ability to meaningfully change the lives of young people.

The systems designed to support young people, which sometimes bring about the kinds of challenges we've discussed, can impact on us. Bureaucracy can be highly frustrating! But let's be clear: you possess the ability to create meaningful change. Please don't doubt it.

All of us want to get up in the morning knowing that everyone is working together to make the world a better place, but it doesn't work that way, does it? The fluctuations within organisations and governments can cause a ripple effect that quickly brings an innovative practice to an end.

When you sit in your office or with your team, what do you see? Do you feel valued? What does your environment offer you and the young people you are keen to support? Where is your team or organisation heading and what does it stand for? Is it really listening to young people, or is it going around in circles?

Some organisations are doing work that has a powerful effect on the world. They embody the kind of thinking and action this book describes. Leaving such an organisation would be counterproductive. But have you already left? Are you sitting alone at home or in some coffee shop wondering what to do next? Many people I have spoken to look for new organisations whose focus and drive matches their own, but you might also think about starting your own grassroots organisation. Many do.

There is one guarantee in life – everything changes, and these changes have a disproportionate effect on the young. There are large forces at play that can create new agendas throughout society that quickly overshadow and eclipse current agendas. These changes can be rapid, moving with the tide of public opinion and political manoeuvring, but the agendas that now occupy public consciousness may once again become shrouded in mystery. They no longer appear to exist. Young people, who are often powerless to resist these changes, fall through the gaps this process creates.

Our desire to reach a place where no one suffers anymore and everyone has a voice remains unfulfilled. While lasting change is possible, it takes a radical shift in our thinking.

Are we prepared to change the way we think? Challenging convention can transform us, too. We can do this within our current teams and organisations.

Most of us choose to work with young people because our work goes beyond the nine to five. We do it because we think it matters. It goes deeper. Even the non-religious among us will see it as a calling. We are often blind to our own insights and abilities, so how can we recognise whether we have a calling?

Here are a few questions that might just reveal the truth.

1. Do you wake up in the morning feeling optimistic, ready for the challenge? And go to bed at night still thinking about your work?

2. Is there a theme running through the decisions you make? One that reveals that you always return to this kind of work in some form?

3. Would you be prepared to take a pay cut if it meant making a bigger impact in the lives of young people?

4. Are you ready to take a risk for what you believe in?

5. Do you love talking about what you do to anyone who will listen?

6. Do you spend your spare time looking for better ways to do what you do and encouraging others to do the same?

It's important to remember that busyness and progress are not the same. If your aim is to make progress but you feel trapped in an environment where people are just busy running around in circles, perhaps it's time for a change.

Finding meaning in what we do is what turns the job into a vocation. When we can see how we're making a valid contribution to the bigger picture, we become motivated intrinsically. If we put money or status first, we'll be on fragile ground.

What motivates you at a deeper level? What motivates you will likely fail to motivate someone else. Think about your current role. Why does it exist? What function does it fulfil? Someone once told me that leaving a job is like removing a fist from the sand. Once the fist is removed, the sand fills in the gap, making it seem as if the fist were never there. He thought he was being clever but it made me feel sad. It's not as though I want everything to collapse when I leave, but I do want to leave a legacy.

What will your legacy be? Young people's lives transformed? New ways of working that bear your name? It shouldn't be about fame or ego, but about making a difference and creating meaning in our lives and the lives of those around us.

Working with so many people across so many professions can be demanding. The strain of our taking on bigger and bigger workloads and seeing young people's pain is clearly evident around us. But what about you? Are you feeling this strain?

We can see in others the signs that things aren't going well, but we inevitably struggle to see them in ourselves. Do you spend a lot of time worrying about the same small things? Do you take your frustrations home? Do you feel that you and your insights are no longer valued? Have you stopped growing and learning? Are you bored? Are you no longer playing to your strengths?

We're often told there is no 'I' in 'team', but we need an environment where we feel we can innovate. There isn't a team in the world that benefits from its members feeling undervalued and powerless.

Your decision

Whether you choose to stay or go, the decision is important. Staying is not a neutral option. If you're staying, start connecting with young people and their families more effectively. Start challenging the systems you work in to offer better opportunities.

I can't tell you what the right decision is. Every choice has its downsides. But maybe reading this will provide the final push you need to leave your current team or organisation – if so, go for it!

Youth organisations need to recognise that many of their workers do what they do because they want to see young people prosper. Every organisation wants this, of course, but I want to encourage you to think outside the box and tap into those organisations that really get it.

Our work is about developing learning relationships with young people, but it's also about developing them with our teams, no matter how big the organisation has become.

Young people need champions. Youth organisations need them too. And champions need the freedom to express themselves and be part of the organisations in a more radical way.

PART THREE

Creating Lasting Change

CHAPTER NINE

How Revolutions Work

As I considered the aims of this chapter, it dawned on me that the idea of revolution can be quite scary. We want to see things change for the better but we like the quiet life. When I speak to others who are trying to transform the lives of young people, they often suggest that what they're doing (such as developing a new project for young people in the care system) is obvious and easy. But it isn't: creating meaningful change is hard and requires us to think differently.

Revolutionary thinking can be found all over society. We're talking about peaceful revolutions, of course. There's no call to arms here – let's get that straight. But all revolutions arise for the same fundamental reason: a social dilemma. And they all carry a sense of urgency because the longer injustice, inflexibility, and insensitivity go unchallenged, the longer people suffer and struggle. Whether you're working with a small community group trying to raise awareness of the plight of young people with Asperger syndrome in the Outer Hebrides, or working to overthrow a corrupt and despotic government in some far-flung country, the principles are the same; it's just a matter of scale. This means we all have a great deal to learn from successful revolutions.

In Chapter Eleven, we'll focus on kick-starting your desire for change, whatever that might look like and whatever your starting point. But for now, let's focus on what lessons we can learn from successful and peaceful revolutions.

In the 1990s Serbia was struggling. It was run by a powerful dictator who ignored the public feeling and parliamentary results, and ruled the country through fear and violence. A handful of determined individuals saw a need to confront and unseat this dictator, but in a way that wouldn't mean losing their lives.

Since then, many other revolutions have followed the principles these individuals developed. They did so by trial and error. Importantly, their work resulted in a set of tried and tested ways to make change possible. It's important to recognise that these weren't extraordinary people. Actually, there are no ordinary or extraordinary people in the world – just people doing ordinary and extraordinary things. By following these principles, you can do extraordinary things, too.

Revolutions often happen because people are suffering and they need mainstream society to think and act differently. They struggle to get their message across and need to find creative and unconventional ways to bring about change.

Revolutions begin because all the established channels for change have been exhausted and nothing has been achieved. Nothing has changed. The pillars of power aren't listening or looking. Revolutions take us out of the box of conventional thinking and into the far more audacious and disruptive thinking required for real change to happen.

So how are revolutions built, and what can we learn?

They start from the ground up. Revolutions start with people like you and me – with people who have the passion to at least start doing something. Ultimately, we won't succeed on our own; we must develop our tribe. Ideas and concerns can incubate for a long time, and then something may happen to change the landscape and you'll find yourself championing the cause of something that resonates deeply with you.

Early on it will be easy to give up because there will always be people keen to tell you you're wasting your time. Not all 'experts' are experts! It's often the people with little vision who shout the loudest. Would Martin Luther King have succeeded if his mum had told him to 'get a real job' and he'd listened? Revolutions make progress when those who have started them connect with people who will offer constructive feedback and nurture the tribe as it grows.

They have a clear vision and help everyone see what's in it for them. If you want other people to understand what you're doing, your vision needs to be clear. You need to know why you're doing what you're doing in such a way that it's easy to share your cause. In time, you and your tribe will become effective at telling your story to various audiences, so that people from all walks of life can discover they have a vested interest in what you're saying. We'll look at how you can do this in the Sixty-day Challenge. We'll explore ways to get your message to stick.

They think big but tend to start small. It's important to think big! But successful revolutions, movements, and initiatives gather force over time. They think about what battles they can win early on, no matter how small, and do just that. These battles act as building blocks and allow your tribe to test ideas before hitting the mainstream head on.

In 1903 the Wright brothers were the first people to successfully fly a fixed-wing aircraft. They began in engineering, working with printing presses and other machinery. They also worked on bicycles, studying balance. They dreamed of building aircraft and creating stable flight – something that hadn't yet been achieved. It was a big dream. They started small, experimented, and went on to transform aviation. Determine what battles you can win early on.

They develop a clear plan. All revolutions need a plan (we'll use one in the Sixty-day Challenge to help develop ideas and experiment with what might work). And the plan must present a clear and robust solution to the social dilemma.

Plans often include clear branding. Revolutions, start-up businesses, and projects designed to support young people have a great deal in common. People need to recognise a symbol or a slogan, something that they can see or hear that enables them to identify quickly with the cause. They want to take you seriously.

Plans also include specific roles for the tribe, and consider how to develop the resources needed to fulfil certain aims. Successful revolutions develop a coherent plan that plays to the strengths of those in the tribe and looks to bring in other skills that might be needed to keep things moving.

They develop effective campaign strategies. Revolutions work best when built around campaigns. They develop schedules that provide effective feedback on how things are going. Early on, revolutions work instinctively. Tribes respond to opportunities as they come. But to take things on effectively, it's necessary to build on and expand the sphere of influence. It's all about keeping the ball rolling and not resting on previous successes.

It's important to remember that good campaigns bring people together under a common cause. Many campaigns learn to operate within clearly defined cycles that leave room for feedback and reflection. Campaigns like this tell an ongoing story but one with a robust evidence and knowledge base.

They use humour. Revolutions are a little like electric shocks. (This was a good opportunity for a joke, but I couldn't think of one.) Not the ones that create distress, but the ones that make you jump and laugh. Humour is at the centre of successful revolutions. It works because it disrupts the mainstream's response to challenge. The revolution that took place in Egypt saw activists hiding MP3 players containing a song challenging the government. The song was played through speakers at full volume. Soldiers were sent to search for them, and they often had to look through rubbish bins.

Humour can work hand in glove with a more serious message, and defuse the kinds of confrontations that ultimately prove counterproductive. After all, we want the mainstream to be our vehicle for success in the long-term. We're not talking about flippant humour. We're talking about powerful humour that dissipates tension. Mark Twain reportedly said that 'the human race has unquestionably one really effective weapon – laughter … Against the onslaught of laughter, nothing can stand'.

They find out who holds the power and they create allies. Through the Sixty-day Challenge, we'll address how connecting with those in positions of power can make your chances of creating real, long-lasting change more likely. What professionals will connect with your message? Who will support you and advocate your cause? The *right* word at the *right* time from the *right* person can help you make real progress.

When you begin to consider gathering this kind of support, you become more audacious in your thinking. You don't see the hierarchy. You see people living their lives: some have their own difficulties and stories to tell but hide them. You see people in positions of power who really want to help. It brings out the best in them. They want to get involved, and they could later become your allies in your struggle...

I remember reading about Bear Grylls, one of the UK's greatest explorers and advocates of the worldwide scouting movement. He described how he was looking to gain funding for a trip to climb Everest. He wrote many letters to Richard Branson and received no response. Then he got braver and went around to Branson's house with some flowers and a copy of his letter. When he rang the doorbell, he wasn't surprised to be told through the intercom that he wasn't welcome. But the front door had been left unlocked by mistake. He entered the house, called out an apology, left the flowers, and ran. While he didn't get any funding from Branson he refused to give in. Not everyone responds to your call for help but for Bear, who ultimately made it to the top of Everest, his perseverance paid off. He found funding from another source. Creating allies takes bravery, and if you don't ask you don't get, right?

They respond to windows of opportunity. Early on in its development, a tribe needs to be highly mobile. It must look for opportunities to make a point, raise awareness, and challenge convention. Windows of opportunity will sometimes open up. Whatever your agenda or message, there are times when the media will be telling a story, or a local event will be planned, that can act as a platform for you to flag up your cause. It might be an opportunity to work in partnership with other groups. It's surprising how movements of all kinds learn to take advantage of opportunities as they arise.

As they expand their sphere of influence they adapt their strategies and reorganise. All revolutionary organisations start small and adapt. As their sphere of influence grows their resources increase and their tribe expands. This means they must manage their growth and strategic direction well.

They learn to speak the same language as the mainstream. We've already discussed how mainstream society has blind spots and often fails to see what is going on. Sadly, it appears not to care, and when change is discussed the organisations and factions involved will want to know what's in it for them. But successful revolutions help the mainstream see that there are huge benefits to be had from changing views and processes. They connect with the mainstream so well in the long run that most people soon grow to understand the benefits. But it's a long road. It's not done in sixty days!

They learn to future-proof their work. Challenging convention is a long journey, and successful revolutionary movements don't stop once the initial aim is reached. They don't leave a vacuum. They finish what they started. But it's all about timing – future-proofing your work demands a different way of thinking. As your tribe grows and changes so will its skillsets. You'll be able to start formalising your approaches as the mainstream starts to adopt them. You'll know when you have future-proofed your work because it will continue even when you have moved. New habits will continue and become embedded and, if you are lucky, you'll see things grow and change for the better.

Young people are struggling within systems and communities that should know better. Like me, you may feel frustrated when approaching the people and organisations set up to help. We've seen how gaps appear and how systems lack the flexibility and sensitivity to really meet a need.

But if we approach the need for change with a determination to create opportunities that will positively alter the life paths of the young people we support, we're onto something good.

We need to think like revolutionaries!

Successful revolutions teach us important lessons. They teach us that big and apparently immovable organisations and systems can in fact be moved by people like you and me. We can do so with a smile and a determination to succeed. It's never easy and can take a long time, but it can be done.

They teach us that you don't have to be an extraordinary person to do extraordinary things. For example, Malala Yousafzai wanted to go to school. She was targeted by the Taliban and left for dead. She survived and now campaigns for young people all over the world. Does she see herself as an extraordinary person? Probably not. It's her bravery that resonates.

They teach us that creating change can be fun and exhilarating. It can often be a long slog, and what can go wrong will likely go wrong. However, if your tribe has a good sense of humour, you'll create goodwill and get on better.

They teach us that you don't have to be loud. Imagine a movement run by people who couldn't speak. How would they get their voices heard? I think they could be very powerful.

Finally, they teach us how people can do amazing things when properly organised.

CHAPTER TEN

The Building Blocks Of The Sixty-day Challenge

Before we get started on the Sixty-day Challenge, we'll look at the building blocks. Together they paint a picture. And behind every painting is a story. Every piece of art is more than the moment you share with it.

We have already seen how the mainstream creates systems with blind spots and organisations that don't communicate effectively. It also struggles to listen to calls for help until something terrible happens and we're placed in the public consciousness. But youth organisations should never work this way. Regardless of their size, they should maintain an openness and agility that means they can respond to the changing needs of young people.

The Sixty-day Challenge was developed to increase our ability to inject greater flexibility and sensitivity into our systems. Its fundamental priority is to develop a greater understanding of the lives of young people, of how the way mainstream society thinks really impacts on them, and of how little we really know. We also need to find clever ways to work in partnership with mainstream and access its resources.

Creating lasting and meaningful change requires far more resourcefulness than we might realise at first. Please note that I'm not talking about resources. The mainstream carries the bulk of the resources, and they aren't worth much if they aren't used well. They don't carry the value they should. Too many resources are in the hands of people and organisations who are unable to exploit them successfully.

One of the fundamental reasons why the mainstream struggles to unlock its resource potential is that it makes assumptions about solutions. I've worked in mainstream organisations. They assume that the solutions to social problems are self-evident and obvious, and if you pour enough resources on these problems, you solve them. Of course this isn't the case – otherwise, the richer nations would have solved all their social problems by now.

The mainstream also assumes there's a menu of self-evident solutions to choose from. Those who have worked in organisations long enough will often see old ideas and 'solutions' resurface (repackaged but clearly the same). It also assumes that having all the resources places you in a position of superiority when it comes to ideas and solutions. Actually, it doesn't. We need to challenge these assumptions.

Our systems are also built upon assumptions that have been proven inaccurate and erroneous over time. For example, 'the poor': mainstream society still views the poor and needy in negative terms, in much the same way as it did a hundred years ago, and will not let them contribute in the present. What about intelligence? What does it really mean to be intelligent? Western schools put a lot of faith in academic intelligence. As a result, many youth organisations have been set up to bridge the gap between what schools teach young people and what the real world expects from them. As adults, we also tend to assume we remember what it's like to be young; we make assumptions about what young people need and don't need. We assume we know what we are preparing them for (good luck there!) and how we should do it. The truth is that we can help a great deal, but to do so, we must first gain a greater understanding of the situation. We must stop and listen, not make assumptions.

True resourcefulness finds its voice in difficult and challenging circumstances. If you're sitting on a big box of resources provided by the mainstream, put it aside for a little while. No doubt it comes with a label detailing its terms of use, and will bear little fruit when it comes to unpacking what the young people you support really need. But it will prove useful once you become truly resourceful.

Imagine you're a millionaire. You're driving your fast car on the outskirts of a Scottish island and you break down.

You have no phone signal and it's getting dark. You think of all the resources at your disposal – an international team of lawyers, six other cars, a driver, an assistant, a motorbike, and a mountain bike – all out of reach. Resources have no value in a challenge like this. I'm not implying that millionaires aren't resourceful. But what would you do in this situation?

The Sixty-day Challenge encourages you to explore the assets you have. The social dilemmas we face require the kind of thinking that mainstream resources fail to encourage. Revolutions thrive amid what may seem like a resource desert. In fact, we have more resources (and better resources) at our disposal than we might think. We'll explore this oasis. The journey may surprise you.

We can also create real value through ideas. Ideas are wonderful things. They often appear in the strangest of moments, and in very different ways. But the process of turning ideas into valuable assets is an important one.

Ideas are like new team members. Though they may smile and seem highly relevant to the task at hand, they are works in progress. We should welcome them and enjoy their company but also be willing to test their loyalty and judge their value, especially after introducing them.

All ideas should be tested. We should never get emotionally attached to them, in case we need to discard them. Creating bespoke solutions to social dilemmas isn't easy.

It takes hard work and commitment. The study of creativity is complex, but certain aspects of it fit well within the ethos of this book. As ideas gain traction and survive the various stages of development, they increase in value. I've broken down the process that ideas go through into five steps.

The five steps

Step one – incubation

If you want to create lasting change in the lives of young people, you've probably been thinking about it for quite a while. You probably have more than one idea when it comes to creating this change, and because you believe a solution is worth fighting for, you will have seen pieces of the puzzle in unusual places. Incubation can go on for years. Evidence of the incubation process will be found in your story. This is why your story is so important. At this step though, ideas have little or no value. They may carry huge potential but aren't impacting on the lives of young people and the systems that support them in any value-laden way. During the Sixty-day Challenge, you can begin to unlock this potential. Often, ideas are locked into teams and entire organisations.

Ideas will always be incubating as you look for potential solutions to various problems that interest you. But as you work through these steps, you'll do so with a particular social dilemma in mind.

Step two – deliberation

Some ideas will leave the confines of your mind and enter the arena of deliberation, where they are laid bare and shared with others. At this step, you share ownership. Ideas created to solve problems begin to line up as potential solutions. They begin to find a place within your 'why' – your mission. As discussions develop and more ideas surface, you will begin to create your hypothesis (that is, 'I believe that if we do "this", the outcome will be "this"').

Step three – experimentation

Once your mission and hypothesis have been thought through, it's time for experiments. Treat these experiments as you would a start-up business (although in some cases you may actually be starting a business!). The campaigns you develop are also experiments with built-in feedback loops that link directly to your attempts to develop greater understanding and learning relationships and to show the mainstream what's working and what could be done better. Young people should always be at the centre of your campaigns.

The aim is to learn as quickly and effectively as possible, to be resourceful and create something that the mainstream can relate to. As your product or approach develops, ideas will still be incubating, and you'll be deliberating others. The Sixty-day Challenge will help you get to this point.

Step four - action

Once you've begun to fine-tune your engine, it's time for action. You want a wider reception for your offering. Your campaign schedule will still present the need to innovate and respond to windows of opportunity, but strategically, you're thinking more long-term and looking differently at resources. Your tribe develops during this period, as different skills may be required.

Step five - separation

There comes a time when what was once seen by the mainstream as an unconventional approach becomes separated from its more radical roots and firmly establishes itself within the mainstream. The young people you support, once marginalised or misunderstood, are now part of mainstream thinking. We're no longer talking about ideas but about fully integrated practices that display greater flexibility and sensitivity.

This is not the end, of course! New ideas are still needed because the mainstream, by its very nature, will carry on making the same assumptions and struggle to generalise any new solutions or strategies. Its response is usually to create a new service or provision, and those working within it will find it hard to think outside of it. We must always create value-laden strategies that directly impact on young people's lives. Our thinking always needs to disrupt and challenge. We want society to do a better job of recognising when it has missed something.

The impact of environment

Nature and nurture have long been two of the key players determining how we respond to life's challenges and opportunities. For example, young people with autism have difficult lives. We see how genetically and neurologically they are gifted with unique insights into the world but also struggle to make sense of the complex web of social interactions, communicative cues, and sensory information bombarding them constantly. I have witnessed so many young people with autism struggle in mainstream settings but then go on to thrive, often as a result of just the smallest adjustment to their social environment.

The truth is that we are all highly sensitive to changes in our environment. We also do everything we can to develop some sense of control over it, and when we can't, we look to challenge and influence it in any way we can. I remember attending a training course on autism. Many of the attendees were senior schoolteachers, including a head teacher keen to increase his knowledge. The tutor was quite rude and insisted that everyone sit quietly and get on with their work. This didn't go down well with the senior teachers, who clearly felt that their status was being challenged. I watched them misbehave and start throwing bits of paper around the room! Our environments can directly affect our behaviour. Our environments are often highly inconsistent and volatile. We must be keen to develop a real understanding of the environments young people are expected to operate in.

We must understand social ecosystems if we are to create opportunities for lasting change. These ecosystems are everywhere. They are our schools and colleges. They are communities defined by their network of human interactions. They are largely self-supporting and interdependent.

Social ecosystems, which young people are wrapped up in, are controlled by both internal factors (long-held cultural beliefs, practices, expectations, roles and responsibilities, etc.) and external factors. The external factors can have drastic effects on the ecosystem, which is often highly sensitive to change. Many of these factors come from the mainstream. For example, we are all too familiar with how new policies and initiatives can cause disruption in schools.

Some ecosystems will resist change. But these can be guilty of conforming to the pressures of external (mainstream) factors, regardless of the consequences – even when given greater freedom to think differently. It's not surprising, as all external pressures leave scars if what's insisted upon causes more harm than good.

All ecosystems are subject to feedback loops. Let's use a school as an example. An educational government authority (external factor), which holds the power, can change these feedback loops. Annoyingly, this authority isn't affected in the slightest by what goes on within individual schools, unless schools start complaining collectively. Even then, the mainstream authorities rarely change their tack. To move forward, we must gain a greater understanding of how the ecosystems function, and what can be done to encourage change, so that young people prosper.

Good ecosystems (those that young people can connect with) are ecosystems of learning relationships. Learning relationships aren't an option: they are a necessity. All hierarchical systems are in danger of creating environments that limit autonomy and opportunities to grow, despite the best intentions.

Once we view a young person as a number or a statistic and lose sight of their humanity, we fail them. We see problems of this nature all over the world, throughout our schools, colleges, prisons, and many other systems.

The Sixty-day Challenge helps you find ways to look carefully at the environment a young person finds themselves in. When we say a young person is 'acting out of character' or that we 'don't know what came over them', we need look at the reasons why and at their environment and how it's structured. The environment plays an important role, particularly when so much is out of their control.

The tribal skill sets

Creating lasting change isn't a solo activity. It takes a group of passionate individuals – your tribe. Like you, the members of your tribe need to fit the profile of a champion. They will connect instantly with your dreams of change, even if your vision isn't fully formed. They will offer something special. They will help you believe in more, and help you focus. And they will provide sets of skills that complement yours.

I've narrowed down the three tribal skill sets that are essential for change. Each is united to the others by its capacity to create connections vital to making change possible. But what sets them apart is the way they do this.

Over the years, I've found that it's difficult to make progress without people who can take on the following distinct roles. But I've also come to realise that having a tribe that manages to fulfil its remit as a team is more important than recognising individuals. Let me tell you more about them.

Specialists

Specialists connect people with ideas, knowledge, and wisdom across various fields and domains. They thrive on gathering information. They cross boundaries and help you frame your ideas and motives effectively. Mainstream society wants to see how your work and passion is revealed in history, how it finds its voice through knowledge and research. Specialists love to show this and are therefore vital to your efforts.

They can see win-win scenarios and help you gain a greater understanding of the key issues. They can be highly creative. This is the first skill set your tribe needs to develop – the ability to connect with a strong knowledge base.

Brokers

Brokers have an inherent ability to connect people with people. They will share your passion for finding solutions to support young people. They love to network. They are well known as givers and people with integrity. Their work is highly regarded by just about everybody.

They will tend to know someone who can help you, and will connect you with them. Good brokers love to tell stories and connect with others at a deeper level. In other words, they are good at sharing messages. This is the second skill set – the ability to connect with people who will get your message. This is important if you are to grow and expand your sphere of influence.

Salespeople

Good salespeople are adept at connecting people with your message and opening doors that encourage people to make decisions. The ability to sell and pitch an idea or message and extol its true value is a real skill. Good salespeople do so with integrity, believing in what they're selling.

They are driven to make a transaction and to see someone commit to action. They don't give up, and can adapt their approach to suit the people to whom they are talking. They understand that people are thinking, 'What's in it for me?' This is the third skill set, which helps your tribe challenge convention and gets the mainstream to act. Without it, you'll struggle to get your message across.

Creating a strong tribe isn't easy, but if you have a clear view of the skills you need to have access to, everything soon falls into place.

Even if you can't identify individuals who can do these three things, your tribe as a whole still needs to be able to do them to be at its most potent:

- ⟲ connect people with ideas, knowledge, and wisdom across fields and domains

- ⟲ connect people with other people able to support your aims and objectives

- ⟲ connect people with your message and open doors that encourage people to make decisions

Throughout the Sixty-day Challenge you'll be encouraged to start developing your tribe. You may already know people who can fulfil these roles – maybe you've just realised this! If not, you'll be on the lookout for them.

One more thing about your tribe. During our discussion about revolutions, we examined how humour can play an important role in breaking down the barriers you'll face. Your tribe needs a joker in the pack, or more than one! If members of your tribe can balance the need to take things seriously but also use humour and creativity to challenge mainstream thinking, all the better.

Evidence indicates that by making the smallest of tweaks, we can help make important changes in the fabric of our societies. It is the collective and focused nature of these tweaks that create value.

Young people don't generally crash and struggle because of some huge event. It does happen, of course, but crashes are generally a result of a collection of small 'nicks'. Not being listened to, a sharp word, anxiety, pressure on top of much bigger issues like illness, loss of a loved one, and homelessness – young people face a full range of difficulties, many going unnoticed. That's why it's impossible to solve social problems with huge resources and generic responses. Only through small things, including listening, giving good feedback, buying someone a meal, creating meaningful connections with opportunities, and advocating, will we help them make progress. We can only help if we understand.

I've heard it said many times – we're using Band-Aids to try to cover a gaping wound. And young people get to the point of crisis because of thousands of much smaller cuts. If we stop and listen, and then do the small things well, we can go on to create lasting change.

The wildfire message

How you share your message is important. You will come across many different audiences. Groups and organisations within the mainstream will ask, 'What's in it for me?' I've said many times that we can fix things only through understanding – only when we can reconnect young people and their lives to the world in which they are growing up. Your message needs to have a firm and clear foundation but be delivered fluidly. It must be delivered creatively but retain its integrity.

Sadly, even the most profound and life-changing messages often go unheeded. There are those who want to change, those who are open to change, and those who are completely immovable. The message you bring needs to tell the truth and have integrity. This will give you the best chance of reaching those who do care, and can help you make inroads into the kind of change you need to see.

Mainstream society tends to resist any uprising, but a wildfire message isn't so easy to extinguish. Let me tell you how it works:

- A wildfire message acts like a human brain. It is fluid and vibrant, and always learning to adapt itself to its circumstances. If things go wrong it adapts its networks to find new ways to fulfil its objectives. It is highly intelligent. Most messages are linear. They fail to adapt and shift their focus when it's required and they rely on repetition, but the wildfire message is designed to be more agile.

- A wildfire message will also spread quietly. It makes no fuss and asks for no fanfare. It goes about its business with real focus, driven by clear aims. It rallies people to its cause, working behind the scenes.

⊙ It is designed to be delivered across many settings and environments at the same time. This means it can start and spread organically. In time, your message becomes part of every language because you deliver it in this way.

⊙ The wildfire message acts like a chameleon. It adapts to its surroundings. It does this to allow new solutions to become part of mainstream thinking rather than to hide.

⊙ It has integrity. It is transparent and honest. It does not rely on subterfuge. If your wildfire message was asked to stand up in a court of law it would be guilt-free. It presents a clear and open agenda, and looks for a win-win scenario.

The Sixty-day Challenge will help you develop your wildfire message. If you want to create lasting change, you need to rethink how your message can spread. Don't worry if you're not there yet; your tribe will give your message traction. Start small but dream big.

The Sixty-day Challenge

It's time to get practical. It's time for the Sixty-day Challenge. The challenge is designed to help you do the following:

- test your assumptions

- find powerful ways of telling young people's stories

- consider how the mainstream is working with the young people you care about

- create a working hypothesis

- think about the tribe you need around you to gain the greatest traction

- develop a pool of ideas and begin to focus on the ones you think are worth trying first

- think about the change you want to see and why

- build and align your tribe

- create your message

- look at your resources and become more resourceful

- launch your first wave

- take advantage of windows of opportunity, and

- review your campaign and keep things moving

The challenge represents the first wave of a campaign that you'll design and test with the aim of embedding new ideas into mainstream services and systems. It's not easy. You don't have a lot of resources, but it's important work. Mainstream society needs creative input but will not admit to being frightened of change. It means we need to be subtle and respect this fear and resistance.

The challenge is presented in five stages.

Stage One is designed just for you, the reader. But there are parts that you can go through with a small group, too. Make notes and think expansively about this stage; it will help you get to the heart of the matter. Speak to others and be prepared to challenge your assumptions and expectations.

Stage Two takes you away from your thoughts and encourages you to connect with your tribe. Get together to explore ideas. The focus at this stage will be gathering as many ideas as possible and then filtering them down. I call this 'idea funnelling'.

Stage Three requires you to nail down which ideas you'll work with first. Build your campaign and design your first wave. Align your tribe and agree on common aims. By the end of this stage, you'll be ready to launch!

Stage Four is when you'll launch your first wave. Watch carefully as things unfold. You will have already decided what feedback you're looking for (this is an experiment, after all). Be open to exploiting any windows of opportunity that present themselves.

Stage Five involves taking time out to consider if these ideas are worth pursuing now or in the future. But it isn't the end. What happens next is up to you. Is it time for the next wave?

How you allocate your time is important. The sixty days will go by very quickly and you will want to get full value from your efforts. While the stages are clearly defined, they will still overlap. It is not easy to meet up with your tribe and be disciplined enough not to talk about a new idea when you are supposed to be thinking through something else, but you need to be focused.

The Sixty-day Challenge is designed to run over two calendar months and can be broken down to eight or nine weeks.

I recommend planning a start date that you can all agree with. Then look forward to consider when you might launch your first wave. This works well if you plan it for week seven, leaving week eight to gather feedback and plan your adjustments for the next wave.

There are some key questions worth thinking through as you plan your challenge. How often will you be meeting your tribe? (Every day? Once a week?) It might be hard getting everyone together. How will you communicate during the sixty days and share ideas?

To give you a rough idea, Stage One will normally last about two weeks. It is important not to neglect this stage because it provides the stories you need to capture and will enable you to hone your message. I recommend getting everyone together as much as possible during Stage One. Please record your ideas and discuss them later. People get ideas all the time, so they are worth recording as they arise.

Stages Two and Three are spread over the next four or five weeks. They will overlap, but that will become obvious as you read though the challenge.

Stages Four and Five run over the final couple of weeks, although feedback rarely presents itself when you want it. However you plan your time, please give each stage your fullest attention and leave time to celebrate your successes!

PART FOUR

The Sixty-day Challenge

Getting To The Heart Of The Matter

Overview

So many of the problems young people experience are a result of the assumptions we make. The mainstream is guilty of assuming what works and what doesn't, and can't make (and often won't make) the adjustments needed to make things better. But that's where you come in.

The first stage of the Sixty-day Challenge is about challenging your own assumptions, and you need to be open to exploring. It's not about finalising your view but about coming up with a working hypothesis. You will go on to test and refine it until a new theory emerges.

Getting to the heart of the matter is never easy, and it only happens when we are open and honest and prepared to admit we might be wrong. Young people need you in their corner. They need you to open doors and tell their stories in powerful ways that force the mainstream to act.

You'll need to immerse yourself in what life is really like for the young people you are looking to support and empower. You probably already know a lot, and your experience will prove that. But you will likely realise how much you still need to learn.

In Stage One you'll:

○ look more closely at your own motives: knowing why we are taking this challenge helps us frame why we're doing what we're doing, and gives us focus when things get tough

○ go deeper into young people's stories: we know stories are powerful, especially if we can tell them in such a way that the mainstream connects with them

○ explore how mainstream systems (like education and healthcare) define and respond to the problems young people are facing, looking at both the internal factors that impact most heavily on their lives and the external factors that make a big difference to outcomes (this will mean thinking differently about the ideas you generate and use later)

○ create your working hypothesis

Let's start with you

To get to the heart of the matter, we need to stop and look at ourselves first. How do we connect with young people? If you're going through this stage in a group, there's a lot to be gained by sharing your motives and expectations with each other. Spend some time on your own too, to reflect on the process as it unfolds.

It is often our own stories that add a dimension to the messages we share. We may have experienced something similar, or know people who have struggled in identical ways. You can approach this over a few days. I encourage you to immerse yourself in this. It's not about pulling up difficult memories but about finding points of connection. What makes you determined to find a better way for them?

To help you think about your own story, try the following exercises:

- ◔ Think of five ways that you identify with young people, keeping your own story as a focal point. You might consider your own childhood or your own children, or perhaps something you've read, or seen on TV. When I do this exercise I often reflect on my childhood and how determined I am to provide the kind of support I needed when I was a boy in school but never actually got.

- ◔ Try the triple 'why'. Write down why you want to help. Then ask yourself why again. Then do it a third time. It's amazing how this will challenge you to consider what's really at the heart of the matter for you.

◉ Consider this: if you had to write a short personal statement (one paragraph) about why things need to change, what would you say? Focusing like this is important, and will help you with your organisation's message later on.

Young people struggle in ways that often surprise us. How do we connect with their stories? How do we describe what is happening? What is our focus? Their stories and the message you end up bringing to the mainstream are deeply connected. We see young people interacting with mainstream society within a social ecosystem, be it a school, a care system, or perhaps a psychology service. But these ecosystems never tell the whole story. What's going on outside? In the home or community? To have a greater chance of success we need to gain a deeper understanding of what young people are going through.

Many established youth organisations and seasoned advocates will have done a great deal of soul searching already, but it's worth stopping and reminding ourselves of what really matters. It's worth stopping and answering the following questions.

What story do our mainstream systems and services tell about the young people at the centre of your challenge?

This is the divide you're hoping to bridge. Think about labels, assumptions, etc. What are they saying? It drives all their policies and practices. Getting to grips with this gets you to the heart of the mainstream's thinking.

How would you describe the gap between what mainstream society thinks it sees and what might really be going on?

Remember that the quicker someone jumps to a conclusion, the more likely it is that this conclusion is wrong. We need to slow down and look more closely. What has the mainstream done wrong? How great is the injustice?

You're sitting in a meeting and have the opportunity to tell a story about your young people. Where do you start?

You need to be the one reading between the lines, where the really important stuff is. But be conscious, too, that in the process you'll learn more than you thought possible.

Are you able to speak to young people directly? If so, what questions will you ask them?

Closed questions that provide more direct answers are often best. Many young people have become so accustomed to conforming to the mainstream that they find it hard to recognise problems, and the ways they have fully accepted social wrongs. Some lack the ability to be assertive and make a point. That's why we're here. (Some young people possess deep insight, so prepare to be amazed!)

If you can, why not have more in-depth conversations?

It's amazing what you can learn by asking the right questions. Make notes and go on to share them with your tribe.

Before you started supporting young people, what five things had you never realised about them?

Take the time to look for them! They are there. Small things make big things happen, and it's often the small things that impact young people's lives the most.

It's time to take a close look at the mainstream systems and services, particularly at how they respond to the young people you're looking to support. It has more resources than it lets on, but these resources are often tied up in complex webs, earmarked for objectives that have no bearing on the lives of the young people. What are the internal factors causing the difficulties you see and hear? Is mainstream society going around in circles? Indifferent? Is there any sign of caring or progress? Remember that our mainstream education and care systems don't get everything wrong – it helps most of the people most of the time. They just have a habit of letting down the neediest who, with a little bit of creative thinking, could lead transformed lives.

We'll start by looking at the ecosystem that impacts most on the young people you represent, and the *internal* factors.

This might be a complex system, but the more you grow to understand all the players, the better you can tailor your ideas later. Once this stage is completed, you'll see far more than before. But it's the process of the campaigns that unlocks a deeper and more refined understanding of the issues, and unsurprisingly, much about the ecosystem is prone to longer-term change.

New people in positions of power, previous allies moving on, and changes in internal policy all have an impact. As do faulty thinking and deep-seated prejudice. We need to gain as clear a picture as possible as to how the structures within the ecosystems aid or restrict both you and your attempt to bring about long-needed change, as well as the young people. Sometimes the ecosystems are completely unaware of the challenges the young people face and can be open to looking at themselves reflectively, but this is rare. Please consider the following questions, designed to help you unpick the true impact of these social ecosystems.

What do the policies and procedures actually say?

These documents (some of which will be legal documents) can provide insight into how the individual mainstream services and systems think and speak. It is often not that hard to see from such documents how they are responding to young people's needs. They reveal the kind of language and terminology they use and the promises they make. They reveal some good intentions and ideas but you will also be able to see the gaps.

How do you think the environment, with its rules and regulations, affects young people's behaviour and well-being?

People rarely look at the broader environment as being important. But young people's environments spread across systems. Spend time thinking about how expectations are shared.

How open to change are the organisations you are dealing with? Do you think they can change?

Mainstream society often struggles to change its view. It can get stuck. Your role is to look carefully at how closed certain parts of the ecosystem are, and consider what it might take for things to tip in your favour.

Who, within the ecosystem, shows that they care, and how do they show this?

You will find advocates within the systems. Are they in a position to influence your movement? Will they stand by you?

Do you have a direct line to those in power who might rally people to your cause both internally and externally?

Who really connects with your cause but also carries authority to allow your innovative thinking to reach new heights? As your message and working hypothesis start to form you will find yourself talking to all sorts of people. You'll know when someone connects with your message. If they are in a position of influence, they will become a useful ally.

How do the mainstream systems you encounter tend to respond when their failings are exposed?

It is not always wise to be the one who reveals their failings! Sometimes I find they can shut down and refuse to co-operate, but at other times they can surprise us and ask for our help. It is not the aim of this book to embarrass people or cause conflict, but we do need to work within and around mainstream systems to ensure young people's needs are being met and understood. Reaction from the mainstream will change how we plan our campaigns.

What resources might be open to you from within the ecosystem?

Think about finances but don't always prioritise them. Consider people and the willingness to change. Try thinking outside of the way mainstream society might do.

What are the biggest external factors?

Who wields the power from outside the ecosystem? The local government? How does the hierarchy work? Take time to explore these factors because to be effective, you'll need to see who holds the power and who answers to whom.

Your working hypothesis

Having spent the time getting to the heart of the matter, consider what you think needs to happen next. Your working hypothesis is a starting point. It's a statement of both your intentions and the outcomes you're looking for.

But it's important to be realistic. We're making predictions in a highly unpredictable world. You will make mistakes. Things won't work out the way you think. Sometimes they will turn out better, sometimes worse. Sometimes you'll be left wondering what on earth just happened. The Sixty-day Challenge encourages you to be more scientific and focused in the way you explore options, but sometimes the world won't let you. It's important to work with a plan and humbly respect the fact that we are always learning.

I once worked with a young man who explained how he would lie on his bed in the quiet every day and imagine a world where he wasn't anxious. He could describe it in detail – how people knew he struggled socially, and how they made every effort to find ways for him to learn while making it all seem normal. There were few surprises. He didn't feel vulnerable even though his body struggled with sensory overload. Over time, the world grew to respect and understand how the environment impacted on his well-being and learned to adjust, thereby accepting him fully.

In our work, we would call this his 'perfect day'. We could frame it in our discussions and work our way backward from it. This is often called reverse sequence planning. After determining what we could change and what we couldn't, we would start making micro-adjustments to his thinking and his environment.

To create a well-thought-out working hypothesis, think about your perfect day, or a perfect day for the young people you're supporting. We need to be realistic but always thinking big. It's one of our rules.

Your working hypothesis may fall short but ultimately lead to something much better. On the other hand, it may succeed and prove highly intuitive.

To create your working hypothesis, follow this simple process. (You can follow the same process when you start developing ideas in Stage Two and go on to design your first campaign in Stage Three.)

Determine the following:

1. a headline (which provides both focus and identity)

2. the need (what are the gaps, problems, and concerns?)

3. the perfect day outcomes (what you need to see)

4. a process (what needs to be done and what over-arching approach do you think will work?)

5. the benefit (for the young people, you, and the
   mainstream)

At this stage, we're thinking big picture. We're not thinking
about how but about causation – simple cause and effect.
That is, if you set out to tell *this* story and start changing
things in *this* area in *this* particular way then *this* will be
the result.

A while ago I worked in a famous school. The school team
began to show a real interest in exploring what life was like
for introverted students. Discussions went on, and a tribe
with the desire to find out grew. We felt that there was a
lot of room to help every student learn to take time out
from all the noise, social media, and pressure to become
more creative and innovative.

We set out our working hypothesis: the Power of Quiet
(the headline). Next, through open discussion, we described
how more than a third of the students were struggling
within the extrovert and socially saturated environment
and would benefit from a series of interventions that we
would look to embed into the mainstream system already
established – to normalise this kind of thinking and way
of working (the need). We imagined a future where those
who needed quiet could find a way to fit in better and work
in an environment that would unleash their full potential
alongside the extroverts (perfect day outcome).

The process would involve raising awareness, helping to
immerse the whole school culture in a new way of thinking

and learning, and creating changes in the environment that would make it easier for the quieter students to prosper on equal terms. This process would be designed to allow everyone to play a part (because to embed something like this, everyone would need to be able to empathise).

We believed that the benefits were many. Students unaware of their differences would become empowered and their mental health would improve, staff would be able to get more out of these students academically, and there would be greater creative input longer term. Plus (being mainstream savvy), we emphasised that exam results would improve because students would be less stressed and more focused!

Sometimes the need will be much more vital – for some, life or death. You may describe the need in specific terms: 'to keep the girls in our community safe from traffickers', or 'to help our minority students gain the same opportunities as other students when they leave college'. These are causes worth fighting for.

It's up to you how you write yours. You can operate within a *mission statement*, or simply write down everything under these five headings, but at this stage, remember the big picture.

You may not know the process at this stage, but you can start thinking about it. Tap into young people's stories and the passion you possess. As each campaign comes and goes, you can develop new working hypotheses. That's fine! Just start.

What next?

If you've completed this phase with honesty and attention to detail, you will be well placed to consider which ideas you can use to test your hypothesis and refine your message. Ready?

For more advice on how to create your working hypothesis, visit johass.com.

Generating Powerful Ideas

Overview

Good ideas can transform young people's lives. The challenge is developing them so they provide maximum value. At this stage, we need to be open to lots of ideas and keep track of them. They can arrive from the most unexpected places and at the most inopportune moments. Have you ever been in a group of people trying to find a solution to a pressing problem only to see someone new walk in, solve it, and walk away?

Solutions will often present themselves, but they need to be tested. This testing is a major part of the Sixty-day Challenge. As far as we're concerned, only ideas that can help us bridge the gaps between young people and mainstream thinking matter. There's no room for ego here because the ideas need the tribe to make them work, and once embedded into mainstream systems, they're not yours anymore. The mainstream system (the social care system, for example) adopts them as their own. That's the aim.

In Stage Two you'll:

- look at your tribe and decide what skill sets are needed to take the ideas forward (both now and in the future)

- start using 'blue-sky thinking', and allowing yourself to think outside normal boundaries

- save your ideas in an idea log (because you never know when you might need them); ideas that might seem silly now can interact with other ideas in the future and result in something truly remarkable

- think about how your ideas will directly affect both the young people and the mainstream, and how they'll bridge the gap between them

- think long-term about the change that's needed

Forming your tribe from the ground up

Ideas as potential solutions often spend a lot of time in the incubation phase. You need to start deliberating them to make them valuable. For deliberation, you need a tribe. Maybe there are only two of you, or you might even be on your own, but there's no time like the present to start thinking about what your tribe might look like. You can't do this on your own.

To gain traction and offer value, your ideas need your tribe, and to bridge the gaps and connect with young people, your tribe needs your ideas.

It's always interesting to see the makeup of tribes, and how they interact. The members of some work closely together on a daily basis while the members of others have specific roles and never meet each other. But at the centre of every tribe is the heartbeat – the one who drives it, the one who connects everybody. And that heartbeat is probably you.

You don't have to be the one selling your message in front of hundreds of people. Some of us struggle with that. You don't have to be the one with all the knowledge. Someone needs to see the bigger picture and pull the people together. So what skills do you already have in your tribe and what's missing? How will you recruit support as you go along? Remember, you're in it for the long haul.

Why not perform a skills audit? You might be amazed at the skills your tribe possesses. The best tribes combine the ability to think on their feet and be intuitive with a formulaic focus. Both are required. Mainstream society follows a formula. You hold all the cards if you can do both.

Finally, how will you involve young people in the process? Their contribution is important. Here are some questions designed to help you evaluate your tribe.

Which members of your tribe fulfil the role of specialist?

Who can connect you with knowledge and wisdom about the issues you and young people face? Who is able to go away and come back with new research or connections?

Which members of your tribe fulfil the role of broker?

Who can connect people with people? Who can see win-win scenarios?

Which members of your tribe fulfil the role of salesperson?

Who can sell ice to the Inuit? Who knows how a good pitch works and can get people to make decisions? Can they teach you how do that? They'll be great at developing a killer wildfire message.

These are specialist roles, but sometimes you'll find people who possess combinations of these skills. You'll also need people who are good at social media, good at graphic design, etc. Artists, writers, and poets all add value to the tribe. Some people in your community may have been working in this area for some time. Do your ideas and aims match? Consider community groups, various professionals, and passionate parents, too. It's important to find people who are givers, those who help without expecting something in return. I've seen people attach themselves to a tribe and drain it of energy because they make it all about them. In a room full of givers, everyone is supported.

In Stage One we looked at the perfect day. This should have helped you develop your working hypothesis. But what change do you really want to see? Which of your ideas might ultimately link together to create a series of campaigns to help you reach your ideal position – one where young people have better lives and are more effectively supported?

Look forward. Look as far into the future as you can and picture a time when the young people you support don't suffer. How is the mainstream reacting to them? How are their voices heard?

Helping your tribe collaborate effectively

The better you get at sharing ideas in such a way that everyone in the tribe can contribute, the more focused and effective the tribe will be. It's not easy playing to the strengths of everyone in the tribe. Some will love working in large groups, and others will prefer to be alone. Some might want to sit around a table, and others will want to walk and talk. It's your responsibility to get the best out of each member. They have signed up for a reason – namely, they have something to offer.

This is why I love idea cards! They ensure everyone can contribute. Many years ago, I sat with a group of professionals about to embark on a new venture. We wanted a one-line 'attention grabber': something that would bring together our mission and values. Not easy! We spent a long time exploring ideas. Nothing dynamic came up. I felt a little frustrated. Then the chairperson suggested we each take a piece of paper, go away, and come back with an idea written on it. Within two minutes I'd nailed it. Someone then asked me why I hadn't come up with the line sooner. I think the reason was that I like to be away from others when considering a response to something. You may have members in your tribe like this as well.

Sometimes a member of the tribe will stand out as the person most skilled at writing things, such as your working hypothesis or your message. You might ask them to go away and do it, and have the tribe meet later to agree on a way forward. Often much more is achieved this way.

Blue-sky thinking – getting in the zone

At this stage, your written working hypothesis will be your guide.

Blue-sky thinking isn't only about developing new ideas, but also about unlocking ones that are already there and ones that have long been overlooked. The tribe has come together because each person has a vested interest in what you're doing, and therefore will have meaty contributions to make.

Blue-sky thinking means putting aside the worries and the 'can'ts'. We must imagine success, free from any sense of convention and restriction. If we don't, many ideas won't see the light of day – they'll be ignored from the outset. And sometimes, they are the very ideas that can transform our thinking. Here are some pointers.

⊘ Start small! Think of ideas that will create a jigsaw with other ideas. You're looking to build something with a strong foundation. Ideas should be geared towards meeting your overall objectives.

⊘ Keep a log or record of your ideas. Go for quantity at this stage – the more the better.

⊘ Write down your ideas on idea cards. They'll be easy to see, and everyone can carry blank cards with them and fill them in when ideas strike – probably when least expected. (You can find idea cards at johass.com, or just make your own.)

⊘ Keep it simple! Don't try to be too clever. The best ideas are often the simplest. And the simple ideas can be the easiest to implement and learn from. Simple can be powerful.

⊘ Don't let current thinking or beliefs limit your ideas. It's important to understand what ideas do the rounds in the mainstream, but to be creative and find a way forward, you must be unfettered by convention.

⊙ Feel free to wander off occasionally, but as much as possible, stay focused on the task at hand.

⊙ Look for connections between various fields and domains. If you're open, it's amazing what you can find. (The Sixty-day Challenge uses ideas and strategies from many domains, including business, economics, and theology.)

⊙ If someone offers an idea, ask them to explain it to you, and write down this explanation in your log and/or on an idea card. Often the reason why an idea has surfaced will enlighten the group further.

⊙ If you get stuck, do something else. Take a walk, have some fun. When you get back, restate the problem and remind yourself why you're there in the first place. What would the young person say?

⊙ Beware the quiet ones! They can often present the problem in new and innovative ways and then go on to transform your campaign. Find ways for them to contribute.

⊙ Write your overall hypothesis and your aims up for everyone to see.

⊙ Consider what other people and groups are doing outside of the mainstream.

It's not easy getting into the flow of creating great ideas. Some of us struggle to sit in groups and share ideas. We can feel vulnerable. Try telling each other funny or embarrassing stories! Research has proven that they reduce inhibitions and create a better flow of ideas. Humour (despite possibly challenging circumstances) is a great catalyst for both generating effective ideas and delivering campaigns. The tribe should connect, and humour is the way to go.

You will find value in places you thought had none.

Finding potential solutions to tough challenges isn't easy. We all know that. We need to work together, understand our roles, and be creative.

Idea funnelling

Before you get anywhere near designing your first campaign, you need to focus on the ideas you want to implement (this can mean ideas you really like that might be used in later campaigns) and the order in which you might use them.

This period of focus also recognises that new ideas will appear and will need recording. It's worth physically laying out your ideas on the table. (The idea cards are great for this!) In Stage Three, you'll form your initial concept based on the work you're doing now.

Funnelling is useful because it helps bridge the gap between the wild and heady days of blue-sky thinking and the more direct planning stages of your campaign. You need to think about ideas that can start testing your working hypothesis.

Can you see an obvious theme or heading for this first set of ideas? Does the benefit present itself clearly?

As you gear yourself towards Stage Three, it's important to have a much clearer view of what ideas you're going to run with. If you do (and it's fine to amend things as you go along) then you can start planning. This is when it gets exciting!

Building Your Campaign And Aligning Your Tribe

Overview

Moving to Stage Three is exciting. Now that you've spent a great deal of time collecting ideas, certain ones may leap out at you. Which ones will you start with and which will you leave for later? Don't be put off by the apparent size of the task – remember, small things can make a real impact, and it doesn't take much for things to tip in your favour. On the other hand, don't expect instant results. They rarely happen.

In many ways, the design of your first wave is also an experiment. It's not just about creating new projects. It's much more than that. It's also about finding innovative ways to tell young people's stories and creating deeper connections between young people and the mainstream systems that support them. In this digital age there is the temptation to go straight to social media. Think instead about how you can make a real difference in their lives through face-to-face learning relationships. This should always be our default approach if we really want to develop our understanding.

Please be aware that you might mess up. You're stepping into the unknown. You might have to explain yourself to the young people you're trying to support. It's important not to make promises you can't keep. Your campaign should always promise 'low' but, if possible, deliver 'high'. If you can include the young people in the campaign, all the better.

In Stage Three you'll:

- start building your campaign, taking and connecting the best ideas to test their ability to enable young people to find their voices

- start aligning your tribe and their skills and then make plans to gather the support you need to give your campaign the best chance of success

- begin to refine your message, which your tribe will be able to share in powerful ways

- look at your resources and what you need to push your campaign forward

- agree on timelines and the feedback you're looking for – remember that each campaign wave is a form of experiment.

Building your campaign

As you start to build your campaign you'll need to think about your long-term aims and how you'll launch your first wave over the sixty-day period. Your message, like your campaign, can spread like wildfire. It's not linear. Your overall objectives might be, but the way you get there won't be. Life is full of surprises, and some of them are even good! However, your campaign needs structure and firm foundations.

Anyone looking to build something long-lasting starts with a good foundation. They dig deep. You laid the groundwork in the first two stages. Now it's time to start building. But how big do you want this to be?

You will have explored the challenges young people face in ever-increasing depth, fully aware that you're always learning, open to being challenged! You will have worked alongside your tribe to begin developing the ideas capable of taking your message forward and expressing how vital change is needed. You will have suggested a working hypothesis designed to reveal the kind of change you think is both needed and possible.

These are your foundations. Once you start building, they won't be obvious to everyone involved. Still, they remain vital to your success. No one in their right mind starts building somewhere else after laying the foundation! You must always remain true to why you started. To continue in this vein, you'll need to start thinking about your wildfire message.

Creating your message

In the last chapter, we looked at what makes a good message. Now it's time to start writing it. Take a good look at your working hypothesis (your cause-and-effect statement). It will remind you of what exactly you're trying to achieve.

Don't forget your message needs to tell the truth. It also needs to show why change is vital. It needs to reveal the social dilemma you see while also presenting everyone with a way forward. If it can do this, then it has a chance of being heard. So, let's construct your message!

There are some important questions to answer if you want to construct an effective message:

- ⊙ What are the key terms you want to use? These can be related to the young people themselves, such as 'in care' or 'anxious'.

- ⊙ What stories can you use as part of your message?

- ⊙ Are there other groups with a similar message? How can you create a more powerful message?

- ⊙ What terms will the systems you are interacting with understand?

- ⊚ Why is your message important? Why is it vital that those listening commit to thinking more deeply about this issue?

- ⊚ Does it encapsulate your campaign?

- ⊚ Does it draw people together rather than expose their failures? (A good message can cause people to reflect on their roles and responsibilities.)

- ⊚ What can people do right now to help support your message?

- ⊚ Does your message tell the truth?

- ⊚ Is it easy for your whole tribe to tell? (It weakens your message when members of your tribe tell it differently and miss important components.)

Your message must be built in such a way that it creates a bridge between the young people you care about and the mainstream systems that you hope, when you are finished, will be able to meet their needs more effectively.

What makes a wildfire message really work is your ability to find a network of ways to deliver it and environments to pitch it in. Your message needs to be flexible so that it can appeal to any audience. You can reveal your message in front of a group of people in a presentation while also putting up posters, arranging a drama sketch, bringing people in positions of responsibility face to face with the young people you are supporting, and writing an open letter to a prospective supporter. Use your tribe to be more creative, but make sure that everything matches your core message. It means every time your message is shared it resonates and is reinforced.

As a tribe, agree on your message and then practise sharing it! The more times you share it, the more refined it becomes. And as any good salesperson will tell you, it needs to include a call to action. It needs to stir people. I like to help those listening realise that they can make a difference. Our job is to show them how.

Let's start building your campaign around your message.

Your working hypothesis will act as a roadmap, or at least reveal your ideal destination. Imagine standing on the shoreline of a river; the mainstream is on the other side. Your entire campaign is geared towards building a bridge over this river, between you (and the young people) and the mainstream. Each new campaign wave is a stanchion. Some bridges need to be very long, and take a long time to build.

To design your first wave, hand-pick your favourite ideas and throw them into action. Do you remember your perfect day? It's an ideal of course, and you need to be realistic, but if you can't look ahead and see something worth aiming for, you'll get stuck.

At this stage, start thinking about your ideas. Hopefully, you have many and the number is increasing. Which ideas are you going to use in your first wave? Which can go into your second or third wave? Start planning and deliberating.

Pool the ideas you need to start testing and using. (Again, the idea cards are great for this.) You're looking to gather support from early adopters – people who will immediately get on board with your message. As your campaign develops, you'll grow to speak the kind of language that the mainstream knows. And as your ideas become more refined, so will your message and the language you use.

For your first wave, you need to think in terms of showing the mainstream majority the huge benefits of taking your message and ideas on board, because young people's lives will be improved if they do.

Here are some of the most important considerations as you plan your first wave:

- ⊙ You're charting a new course, travelling in virgin terrain, so keep your message/vision in view to stay on track.

- ⊙ You need to take the young people with you. It's all about them, after all. It's not about your fight against the systems.

- ⊙ Your ideas might initially scare the mainstream because the unconventional can sound like another language.

- ⊙ You will need to suggest small changes to the environment.

- ⊙ Through your work, young people must be able to increase their own sphere of influence.

- ⊙ You may not be well received, even though what you're doing is of great value and vital.

- ⊙ Remember, it's about the ebb and flow; like a boxer, you need to keep moving.

Here are some questions to help you with your planning:

- ⊙ Which ideas will you test-drive over the next sixty days?

- ⊙ When and where will you deliver your plan?

- ⊙ How much time will this wave run for? A day? A week?

- ⊙ What resources do you need? How will you be resourceful and creative?

- ⊙ What support can you canvass for both your ongoing campaign and the first wave?

- ⊙ What outcomes are you expecting?

Aligning your tribe

As you prepare your campaign and everyone gets excited, it's important to keep a tight rein on who does what. You need to be well co-ordinated. Mainstream society is watching. You will get a better response if you can keep your tribe together and be as professional as possible. If you have members likely to go off-piste, think carefully about how they'll be involved. I don't recommend taking on everyone who shows an interest. Instead, think carefully about the road ahead and the people you need. If you wouldn't employ them, don't ask them to volunteer. If they're part of an already-established team, manage them carefully. The young people come first.

Again, before you launch your first wave, be clear about who is doing what. It sounds obvious, but I've seen campaigns get off to a bad start because they're badly organised or some member of the tribe shares the wrong message.

It all revolves around your working hypothesis. Built into this is your cause-and-effect statement. This is what you're testing through your initiatives. Think about it this way: if you implement an idea at a particular time in a particular place in a particular way, what should the result be? And the big question is this: how will you know that your ideas, when implemented, will make young people's lives better?

You need to be able to answer the question.

Here's an example. Imagine I'm planning an event with my tribe to raise awareness of the plight of young men in the care system who struggle with mental health issues. We've spotted that the mainstream social care system hasn't connected with their real needs and is, therefore, causing the situation to worsen. We've worked hard to connect with the young people, learned to tell their stories and come up with some brilliant ideas and potential solutions to share with the mainstream system. We've explored how local policy documents the issues and we've refined our message. We might start with an event to connect the social care professionals directly with the young men's plight through a drama workshop and talks by the young people themselves. We might distribute leaflets and a video developed by the young people. But we don't stop there. We plan wave after wave. We find multiple ways to share our message and solutions until the social care system gets used to the ideas and begins to adopt them.

Our working hypothesis might simply be this: 'That if we deliver all these things we should start to see the social care professionals become more empathetic and think differently about their processes and interactions. Young people will begin to achieve better results through the systems, and the systems themselves will start to think more long-term about the young people's lives. They'll develop more effective policies to capture what they have learned. We want to see signs that the social care system is now thinking about how to treat young people in a more bespoke fashion, so each young person is seen as an individual.'

We'll then start to get feedback from the young people themselves. We want to hear them say they're being listened to. They may say that staff are going back to what they used to do. In this case, we'll need to carry on sharing our message in new ways. We'll ask the social workers directly what they've learned. We'll encourage them and provide solutions, always sharing our message until they start sharing it themselves and they have joined our tribe.

Try to remove emotion from your feedback loop. You don't need people telling you that your event was fun and they'll start thinking differently from now on. It's not enough. You need to create ways for the mainstream to change and take over. It's not easy creating an effective feedback loop, but once you have, you can launch your first wave.

Launching Your First Wave

Overview

Imagine you're sitting on the beach as the tide comes in. A wave approaches the shore, makes its mark, and then recedes, as if gathering itself for its next approach. The next wave comes a little closer to you. That is how the campaign process works. Each wave expands your sphere of influence.

In this stage, you'll launch your first wave. And you can go through the same process again and again, building each wave on the previous one. This is the action stage. You and your tribe will be actively involved, watching out for windows of opportunity.

The first wave is different from the rest because it's the first real outing for your message, and a test of your working hypothesis. It's a chance for you to watch and listen. But don't be afraid to ask questions as you do.

In Stage Four you'll:

- learn how to deal with new people wanting to get involved and about the importance of keeping a tight rein on the tribe

- ◎ run your campaign at the launch stage

- ◎ take advantage of windows of opportunity and monitor how things are going

Launching your first wave always involves mixed emotions. You may wonder: How will it be received? What if we don't deliver it as planned? How do we keep our feet on the ground if things go well the first time? The important thing is to just get started.

As I write this, I'm supporting a tribe starting to highlight the need for their school students to have quiet time during the day. This week, they're launching their first wave. They've gained the support of senior figures, who are using their authority to set the scene and have agreed to let the first two initiatives run for a week. Afterwards, the tribe will get together to consider what worked and what didn't. It is a well-planned affair, and they have a good idea of what benefits they want to be seeing.

It'll be the same for you. You've put in the hard work, and now it's time to let it run its course. Whatever happens, it will leave a mark. As the wave unfurls, you might be directly involved or others might be taking the lead. If you're like me, you'll be waiting for the first early signs of feedback. You may even start calling round to find out how it's going.

It's always good to keep your finger on the pulse. This way, you'll be more aware of windows of opportunity. Sometimes, in the midst of a well-run campaign, opportunities to share your message that weren't there before will present themselves.

So how do you take advantage? This is where you and your tribe need to be brave. Working in a small group will ensure you're more fleet of foot, able to respond to these opportunities. Running a campaign is like knocking on lots of doors at the same time, not knowing who might respond, and how. Your message (and the young people's stories) may connect with others in unexpected ways. Doors may open because people have heard about what you're doing.

My dad told me how, as a boy, he'd spend ages tying pieces of string between door knockers across the road from each other. There weren't many cars in those days, but when one did come along, all the knockers rattled at the same time. He once managed twenty doors! All the neighbours came out at the same time, wondering what on earth was going on. My dad certainly got their attention. (You'll be looking for a more positive reaction longer term, of course!)

I do hope your launch includes some fun, too.

As your first wave rolls along, other people will be keen to get involved. This can be both good and bad. A while back, I came across a charity whose aims and objectives appealed to me. It was good working with them on their projects because they recognised my skills and the value

I could bring. I was able to add to their tribe's skillset and helped to spread and refine its message.

As a tribe, you need a clear view of any gaps in your skill set, and you also need to be able to find the best roles for interested parties. You need to test their motives. Managing other people's expectations isn't always easy, but it's worth the effort.

There's nothing worse than sitting at a table with thirty strangers who all want to give their opinions and ride roughshod over your message and expectations. Everyone needs to play a specific part.

Is your campaign up and running? Nearly there? Let's look at how we can learn as much as possible from the experience.

Reviewing
Your Campaign

Overview

So you've started looking more deeply at what's really going on in the young people's lives, and have started to monitor the way the mainstream systems you are working with are responding. You're more aware of your tribe, of its strengths and weaknesses, and have begun to refine your message. Your first wave is complete, but you may have mixed feelings about it. Now is the time to be honest with yourself and look at what worked and what didn't.

Don't be fooled by good feedback early on. The mainstream is fond of flattering such endeavours and making you think you've made your point and they will 'take it from here'. But they struggle to do that, because it takes a lot of time for things to really change. A successful campaign is like water. It wears down rock and reshapes the landscape. So, it's important to keep a professional head on when evaluating your first wave.

In Stage Five you'll:

○ take a rational view of what's worked and what hasn't

○ determine which ideas to take forward as they are, which to tweak, and which to discard

○ find ways to show the mainstream the impact you've had on both their bottom line and in young people's lives

○ review your working hypothesis and look closely at your message

○ get feedback from your tribe and determine how their skills can be used better next time

Your first wave has come and gone. You've put a lot of time and energy into making this work. With your tribe, you will already be thinking and talking about the various components, how they were planned and delivered, how they were taken on board or, perhaps, misconstrued. Waste nothing. Everything is of use. My friend is well known for being able to get every morsel of food off a plate, even when everyone else would have given up. You need to be like this.

The truth is, you've invested a lot of yourself in this. The kind of feedback you'll get and need is rather like someone telling you your house is a mess and needs redecorating. If you ask a question, expect an honest answer. The result is that you'll get a firm grasp of what just happened and what needs to happen in the future. The process may be tough and business-like, but it's vital.

Think about it from the perspective of the young people; they need to know your work isn't about vanity but about them, about their futures and their well-being.

What's worked and what hasn't? It is an interesting question but not as black-and-white as it might seem. Even if an idea is great, what we're evaluating is *how* we delivered it. We're also looking at *who* delivered it and when.

It's up to you how you deliberate, and who is with you when you do, but it's worth going somewhere quiet and leaving yourself plenty of time. You need to look closely at exactly what you did, what people are saying about it, what ideas they might have to improve things, etc.

You'll need to acknowledge what ideas have failed outright and need to be discarded. Maybe the timing was all wrong and they're best left for another time and place. Most ideas will probably need tweaking. That is, you'll need to take the original concept and find other ways to present it. Start-up businesses will often develop an initial idea and design three or four versions of it. This way, they can test it with different groups. You may want to do the same as you go through the many waves of a campaign and discover receptive settings.

I encourage groups to think about both the individual ideas being trialled and the collective nature of the wave when they consider what has been achieved. Have you really begun to test your working hypothesis?

Setting time aside to think clearly is important. What has excited you? How does it make you feel as a tribe? Remember, you're setting out to provide young people with the best possible benefits. Have you begun to tell their story? What have you learned?

This process will also bring up some new ideas and will often resurrect old ones. All of them are worth writing down in your log or on your idea cards. One wave needs to follow the other as smoothly as possible.

We need to remember that we're doing all this because mainstream society hasn't recognised the need. They may have been receptive this time – or not! How will you highlight the real benefits? What's in it for them?

Offering the school or health service a list of benefits can help you gather force and increase your sphere of influence. Any campaign should expand into mainstream society and aim to become fully integrated. I've often found that the mainstream is happy to fund good ideas if you talk to the right people – as long as your efforts put them in a good light! The trick is in your ability to take them along with you. If you can make it look like it's their idea, all the better. If you're in this for fame, find another game. If you want to see young people gain traction and recognition for their strengths and true abilities, carry on!

You'll need to think about your message again. Does it still hold true? Are you more convinced that it's vital you continue? I always encourage tribes to get together and remind themselves of their important message. How well have you all begun to spread your message?

Your message will become clearer due to the simple act of starting the journey. The mainstream needs to hear your message and needs to hear young people's stories. It is vital work.

Afterword:
Thinking Outside The Box

If you were to research the many youth organisations that exist in the world, you might be astounded. Many operate in the most trying circumstances, often saving young people from death and abuse. Children and young people are often lost in the systems and remain invisible to most of us. But many young people are brought back from the brink because people like you and me care. Many lives are recovered. Don't give up and don't stop – because every life matters, and no contribution is ever too small.

Unconventional thinking is required for the kind of work that save lives and unlocks potential. Solutions don't come in neat boxes. Mainstream society is a tough nut to crack. Youth organisations need to remain agile and open to change. They need to continue connecting with young people where it really matters.

In order for youth organisations to retain their integrity and maintain their focus I think they need to do the following:

- ⊙ stay true to their creative and experimental roots – no matter how large an organisation becomes, it needs to maintain a childlike, adventurous spirit

- ⊙ set an example to the wider world

- ⊙ tell young people's stories effectively and be at the cutting edge of youth culture

- ⊙ be open to change

- ⊙ offer a voice of reason and clarity in the darker places of this world

- ⊙ nurture the talents of their champions and give them a voice

- ⊙ be prepared to go the extra mile and to cross boundaries to reveal the challenges young people are really facing

Change is inevitable but feared by many. Mainstream society will always struggle to think like you. In the best-case scenario, it will assimilate new ideas and processes so that young people can't fall through the gaps. The irony is that once an idea is 'owned' by the mainstream, the free thinking that got it there is often no longer required.

As part of a youth organisation, you know how important it is that you continue to innovate. Your ideas will grow.

They will become initiatives. They will be tested and refined and, one day, if we get things right, mainstream society will accept them into their systems. But it shouldn't stop there. Don't give up until you've seen bridges built. Continue looking carefully for new opportunities. Young people need youth organisations to carry on thinking outside the box. They need you to stay agile and alert because their lives are often caught up in the ever-changing social and political landscape. You need to speak up for them and you need to be ready to go out and do what it takes to help unlock their potential.

I hope this book resonates with you and your organisation. I would love to hear the story of your journey. Why not visit johass.com and share it? I plan to publish these stories so others can be inspired, too.

Acknowledgements

I'd like to thank the many young people who have graced these pages and the countless others who haven't. I can see your faces. It's your journeys that matter and your stories that everyone should hear.

I would also like to thank the champions. You know who you are. You have helped me believe in better and given me the courage to challenge others. You know I'm scared and like the quiet life, but you've pointed out that I should be willing to lead the way.

Finally, I would like to thank my wife and children for their support. Everyone thanks their family, but now I know why.

The Author

John has worked with young people for more than thirty years. His career has taken him across the globe, from the US to Russia. During this time, he's had hundreds of discussions with young people, parents, professionals, and youth organisations.

He has worked in education settings with young people struggling to cope, managed youth centres, and advised young people on their careers. He has worked with young people on the autism spectrum, liaised with police forces, helped young people in mental health units, and worked in residential settings. He has also managed teams and developed new ways of working that have become absorbed into mainstream thinking.

He still works one-to-one with young people and is helping a growing number of youth organisations connect with the young people they support, including charities, schools, and new initiatives. In the process, he brings people together, challenges their thinking, and helps them generate powerful ideas.

He is based in the UK and lives with his wife and two children.

🌐 johass.com　　🐦 @johnjohnhassall